D0603806

Managing Crises before They Happen

Managing Crises before They Happen

What Every Executive and Manager Needs to Know about Crisis Management

Ian I. Mitroff

with Gus Anagnos

AMACOM

American Management Association

New York • Atlanta • Boston • Chicago • Kansas City • San Francisco • Washington, D. C.
Brussels • Mexico City • Tokyo • Toronto

Special discounts on bulk quantities of AMACOM books are available to corporations, professional associations, and other organizations. For details, contact Special Sales Department, AMACOM, a division of American Management Association, 1601 Broadway, New York, NY 10019.
Tel.: 212-903-8316 Fax: 212-903-8083
Web site: www.amacombooks.org

Acknowledgments for permission to use previously published materials can be found on page 165.

Library of Congress Cataloging-in-Publication Data

Mitroff, Ian I.
Managing crises before they happen : what every executive and manager needs to know about crises management / by Ian I. Mitroff.
p. cm.
Includes bibliographical references and index.
ISBN 0-8144-0563-0
1. Crisis management. 2. Communication in organizations. 3. Strategic planning. I. Title.

HD49.M5678 2000
658.4'056—dc21 *00-030632*

Printing number

10 9 8 7 6 5 4 3 2

". . . Humans regularly behave in ways they do not well understand, which cause pain to themselves and others, which violate their best understanding of what they want and what they care about."

Jonathan Lear, *Open Minded: Working Out the Logic of the Soul* (Cambridge: Harvard University Press, 1998), p. 54.

Contents

This book is dedicated to my good friend and colleague

Ralph Kilmann

Preface

For most of my adult life, I have studied people working in and around organizations. I have studied them primarily for the purpose of helping them improve so that they could serve themselves, their customers, the environment, and their surrounding communities more responsibly.

I have witnessed firsthand the behavior of individuals and organizations in good and in bad times. I have seen how they function both in normal and in abnormal situations. I have especially studied how they behave in extreme crisis situations.

Nothing better reveals the mettle and the character of a person and an organization than how they respond to a major crisis. Also, nothing better reveals the basic beliefs that individuals and organizations have about human nature than a major crisis.

This book is about the general philosophy or the "bigger picture" of crisis management (CM). It is also about the details of CM. It differs from the vast majority of existing books on CM in that it presents the details within the context of "the larger or bigger picture." This is because, as my colleagues and I have observed again and again, the details of CM are relatively easy to master and even to implement. But this is so *if and only if* one first understands the general, overall philosophy of CM. For example, the fact that many organizations have developed extensive plans and procedures only increases their frustration when they find that they are still not adequately prepared for many crises.

It is absolutely necessary to understand the larger picture because if CM is anything, it is systemic. In other words, crises do not happen merely because a single part of a complex system fails. Rather, they occur because a significant amount of the overall system fails. Thus, CM *is* inherently the process of seeing and dealing with larger, whole systems.

The real, underlying source of the difficulties in implementing a comprehensive program of CM is that it goes sharply against the grain of current management thought and practice. The basic or the most central problem is that it requires cultural acceptance, and unfortunately, in the vast majority of cases, major cultural transformation.

This does not mean that installing a comprehensive program of CM is impossible. Indeed, this entire book argues that the task is imminently doable. The task may be difficult and it may demand enormous commitment, but it is not impossible.

—I. M.

Acknowledgments

The number of people to whom I am indebted in writing this book is too large to mention. However, I would like to single out my good friend and colleague, Warren Bennis. Warren's wise counsel and thoughts are always a deep comfort. I would also like to acknowledge the many conversations I have had with Jean Lipman-Blumen. Needless to say, this book would not have been possible without the constant advice of my good friend and colleague, Ralph Kilmann, to whom this book is dedicated.

Managing Crises before They Happen

Chapter One

Why Crises Are an Inevitable and Permanent Feature of Modern Societies

> "There are no whole truths; all truths are half-truths. It is trying to treat them as whole truths that plays the devil."
>
> Alfred North Whitehead, *Dialogues*, 1953.

Since 1900, twenty-eight "major" industrial accidents have occurred worldwide, with "major" meaning fifty or more deaths.[1] The most disturbing part of this statistic is that half of the twenty-eight have occurred in the past fifteen or so years. There has been a sharp increase in the sheer number of accidents, and the time between them is shrinking dramatically.

In 1982, five persons died from poisoned Tylenol capsules. It was a landmark event because it was the first time that a major pharmaceutical product had been poisoned without prior warning. The perpetrators were never caught. The parent company, Johnson & Johnson, handled the situation so well that they became the standard for crisis management (CM). Indeed, the modern field of CM is generally acknowledged to have started with the Tylenol poisonings.

Crises have become an inevitable, natural feature of our everyday lives. Hardly a day goes by without the occurrence of a new crisis, or the unfolding—better yet, the "dragging on"—of old ones. In other words, crises have become an integral feature of the new information/systems age.

If there are any doubts whatsoever that crises have become a permanent and a prominent feature of our lives, they are quickly dispelled by the following list. The names and the particular crises with which they are associated have become so familiar by now that it is no longer necessary to spell their exact details:

- Mad cow disease
- Nike
- Kathy Lee Gifford (child labor)
- Orange County
- ValuJet
- Columbine
- TWA Flight 800
- Swiss Air 100
- President Clinton's impeachment

Although these recent crises are important, the names of some crises that occurred even earlier have become so well ingrained in our collective psyche that they have become icons:

- The Three Mile Island nuclear disaster
- The Challenger explosion
- The Tylenol poisonings
- The explosion of Union Carbide's chemical plant in Bhopal, India
- The Exxon Valdez oil spill

In short, crises are no longer an aberrant, rare, random, or peripheral feature of today's society. They are built into the very fabric and fiber of modern societies.

All of us everywhere are impacted daily by crises large and small. As a result, all of us, whether we work in large organizations or not, need to understand why crises have become integral features of today's world, and what, if anything, can be done to lessen their impact. We also need to understand what can be reasonably demanded of large organizations so that they can be made as safe as possible, and hence, lower their potential for major crises as much as possible.

Crises are no longer an aberrant, rare, random, or peripheral feature of today's society. They are built into the very fabric and fiber of modern societies.

This book is the result of my more than thirty years' experience in studying complex systems and applying that knowledge to messy problems in business and not-for-profit organizations, as well as numerous government agencies.[2] In particular, since the Tylenol poisonings in 1982, my colleagues and I have helped to found the field of CM.[3] We have studied virtually every kind of crisis imaginable. In addition, we have also advised American and European companies, as well as major government units around the world, on how to prepare for and manage crises more effectively. In the process, we have become privy to some of the most critical and reveal-

While not all crises can be foreseen, let alone prevented, all of them can be managed far more effectively if *we understand and practice the best of what is humanly possible.*

ing information about leading organizations and institutions around the world.

What Is Crisis Management?

In contrast to the disciplines of emergency and risk management, which deal primarily with *natural* disasters, the field of CM deals mainly with *man*-made or *human*-caused crises, such as computer hacking, environmental contamination, executive kidnapping, fraud, product tampering, sexual harassment, and workplace violence. Unlike natural disasters, human-caused crises are *not* inevitable. They do not need to happen. For this reason, the public is extremely critical of those organizations that are responsible for their occurrence.

As a result of our work, my colleagues and I believe that we have developed one of the best and most powerful frameworks for understanding why crises occur in the first place, and what can be done to manage them better before, during, and after their occurrence. (This framework is the subject of Chapter Three.) Nonetheless, even with the best of frameworks and the best of preparations, it is unfortunately still the case that not all crises can be prevented. This even holds true for those crises that we know with almost complete certainty will occur. But the impacts of all crises can be lessened if one has a thorough understanding of the "essential basics" of CM. While not all crises can be foreseen, let alone prevented, all of them can be managed far more effectively *if* we understand and practice the best of what is humanly possible.

What Is Different about Today's World?

What is it about our modern information/industrial society that makes it more prone to crises? And, in particular, why have human-caused crises escalated especially in the last twenty years?

The vast majority of organizations and institutions have not been designed to anticipate crises or to manage them effectively once they have occurred. Neither the mechanisms nor the basic skills are in place for effective CM. Most fundamental of all, the managers and executives of most organizations and institutions still do not understand the "new management and thinking skills" required to head off crises.

What's tragic is that these new skills are not esoteric. They can be taught directly and simply. They are also some of the very same skills that are needed for success in the new global economy.

CM is broader than dealing with crises alone. It provides a unique and critical perspective on the new management skills and the new types of organizations that will be required in the twenty-first century.

Many organizations still think of CM primarily as an exercise in public relations. They feel that the media unfairly manipulate unfortunate events, thus making them into major crises. More to the point, they feel that the media are actually a cause of crises for organizations. From this perspective, the problem is to communicate effectively with the media *after* a crisis has occurred. These same organizations feel that preparing for the media is all the protection they need. While "crisis communications" is certainly an important aspect of effective CM, it is not the whole of it. Effective CM involves much more.

Signal Detection

For instance, signal detection is one of the most important components of CM. Long before they actually occur, virtually all crises send out a repeated trail of "early warning signals," announcing the probable occurrence of a crisis. If these early warning signals can be picked up, amplified, and acted upon effectively, then many crises can be prevented before they occur, which is the best possible form of CM. As a result, all organizations need to constantly scan their entire operations and internal and external environment for early warning signals of potential "ticking time bombs" (latent defects) before it is too late to correct. In short, they need to shift from being *reactive* to being *continuously proactive.* The slogan "If it ain't broke, don't fix it" needs to be replaced with a new attitude: "If it ain't broke, it soon will be; therefore, fix it now when you can still be the good guy, or fix it later and risk being labeled the bad guy."

Denial

In the end, the main enemy, the main barrier to be overcome, is denial. Far too many organizations mouth the cliché, "It can't happen to us; therefore, we don't need to spend the money to prepare for crises." They are wrong, dead wrong!

> *The main enemy, the main barrier to be overcome, is denial.*

But denial is being overcome by the steady increase in the number of crises, which makes it harder and harder to put our heads in the sand. To those of us who work in the field of CM, the issue is not whether an organization will have a string of major crises, but rather *how, when,* and *why* a string of crises will occur, *what form* they will assume, and *how prepared* an organization is to handle them.

Denial is also being overcome by the growing number of model organizations that are doing their best to be better prepared for major crises and thus to manage crises before they occur.

Strategy List for Chapter One

- Recognize that crises are an inherent part of modern societies.
- Realize that man-made crises are avoidable.
- Contemplate forms of signal detection to constantly scan the environment.
- Overcome denial—the worst enemy of crisis management.

Chapter Two

The Failure of Success

The Tylenol Poisonings, Crisis Management's "Ancient History"

". . . as increasingly complex subsystems are linked together—whether they are circuits on a Pentium computer chip or households on a national power grid—there is no way anyone ever can completely understand what has been created and the myriad ways it may fail. It is possible . . . that many of the systems in which the public places its trust have grown too complicated and expensive to ever be made completely reliable. The best that engineers can do is attempt to design these systems to fail safely. . . .

'The whole West is a warren of interconnected transmission lines. *The power grid in the West is the largest machine that man has ever made*—stretching from Canada to Mexico, from the Pacific Coast to the western front of the Rockies,' said Karl Stahlkopf, Vice President for Power Delivery at the Electrical Power Research Institute (emphasis added).

But like any machine, like your lawnmower or your computer or your car, it is susceptible to breakdown."

Robert Lee Hotz and Frank Clifford
"A Glitch in the System," *Los Angeles Times*[1]

Although it is "ancient history," at least as far as crisis management is concerned, it is still important to review the first case that put CM on the map. It is important to review the two Tylenol crises for the CM lessons that were learned and those lessons that were not learned but should have been.

The Tylenol Crisis, 1982

Jim Burke, CEO and chairman of the pharmaceutical giant Johnson & Johnson (J&J), strode briskly to the podium. He was the epitome of confidence and success as he spoke to J&J's top executives at their annual strategic planning conference early in September 1982. He beamed with pride as he noted how lucky they were to be in an industry that had such profitable products. In particular, Tylenol, one of J&J's main brands, had an incredible 37 percent of the billion-dollar analgesic market. Tylenol was so significant that it accounted for an estimated 7 percent of J&J's worldwide sales and from 15 to 20 percent of its total profits in 1981. McNeil Pharmaceuticals, the subsidiary of J&J that actually made Tylenol, was so confident of its success that it predicted that Tylenol would capture 50 percent of the market by 1986.

Smiles of approval spread easily and quickly throughout the room. They had every reason to gloat with their boss. But then suddenly, for some strange and unexpected reason, Burke mused aloud, "What if something happened to one of [our main products] like Tylenol? Nothing is impregnable."[2]

Burke was playfully but forcefully shouted down, for nothing could dampen the spirit of an extraordinarily successful business. Indeed, Burke "took some kidding . . . for worrying about things [he didn't] have to."[3]

There was of course no way of knowing at the time that Burke's musing was an eerie premonition of a nightmare to come. Since modern CM had yet to be invented, the idea that all crises are preceded by early warning signals couldn't have been discussed. And even if it could, how could one have possibly viewed Burke's musings as "early warning signals?" Musings or intuitions are hardly a basis for action in supposedly rational institutions.

Barely three weeks later, on September 29, 1982, two brothers, Adam and Stephen Janis, and Mary Kellerman, of two different suburbs outside Chicago, died after taking Extra-Strength Tylenol capsules. Cyanide, a deadly poison, had been injected into the capsules. A day later, Mary Reiner and Mary McFarland, also of the Chicago suburbs, died of cyanide poisoning. Tylenol was identified as the culprit in their cases as well. Specifically, poisonous capsules were traced to manufacturer's lot number MC2880. Even worse, later deaths would be traced to additional lots 1910MD and MC2738. The utterly unthinkable had occurred. Not only had somebody injected Tylenol with poison, but, worst of all, nobody knew how many different lots had been infected.

J&J reacted promptly. All 93,400 bottles of lot number MC2880 were recalled immediately. A day later, 171,000 bottles of lot number 1910MD were also recalled. On October 4, 1982, the Federal Drug Administration ordered its nineteen laboratories to begin testing Extra-Strength Tylenol capsules. The capsules were drawn from a nationwide random sample from store shelves.

That same day, the widow of Adam Janis filed a $50 million lawsuit against J&J. Two other suits were filed later asking for damages of approximately $35 million dollars. Most severe, a fourth suit was filed demanding that refunds be granted to everyone in the country who bought Tylenol that year! Estimates of the potential cost ran as high as $600 million dollars.

On October 5th, the poisoning had spread across the nation. Three bottles of Extra-Strength Tylenol laced with strychnine were found in Oroville, California.

On October 6th, J&J sent telex messages to approximately 15,000 nationwide retailers and distributors. The messages asked them to remove 11 million bottles of regular and Extra-Strength Tylenol from their shelves.

The initial cost to J&J was measured in more than dollars. The tragedy took its toll in psychological impact as much as in dollars. It affected the confidence and the security that J&J executives had in their own products as much as it did the public's confidence. For the executives of McNeil and J&J, it was like a death in the family. The very foundation of the analgesic business was built on a single, central notion: trust. People took Tylenol because their physicians recommended it or because it was given to them in hospitals. They took it because, in Burke's words, "they were not well and [they were] in a highly emotional state."[4]

As *Fortune* writer Thomas Moore put it: If emotions were responsible for the initial taking of Tylenol and the subsequent brand identification with it, would those same emotions turn against Tylenol because people wouldn't want to take a chance with a product whose name was now emotionally charged in a negative sense? If the name Tylenol was initially associated with goodness and trust, would it now be associated with distrust and evil? After all, who could blame the public for being reluctant to risk its trust? [5]

The questions were not unwarranted. In one of the spookiest and least known aspects of the entire episode, so many people had bet on the numbers of the withdrawn lots—1910, 2738, and 2880—that those numbers had to be closed down in the New Jersey and Pennsylvania state lotteries! The numbers were oversubscribed. People were literally betting that the evil associated with the withdrawn lots would somehow reverse itself and turn to good luck!

The case of Tylenol is an important example of an organization assuming responsibility for its products without being forced to do so.

Although it was strongly advised by both the FDA and the FBI not to recall its bottles in the fear that it would only encourage copycats, J&J nonetheless recalled some 31 million bottles, with a retail value of over $100 million dollars. In other words, J&J *assumed responsibility* for the safety of consumers even though it was not responsible for the poisoning of its products. The case of Tylenol is thus an important example of an organization assuming responsibility for its products without being forced to do so.

As the result of recalling 31 million bottles, J&J's third quarter earnings dropped from 78 cents a share in 1981 to 51 cents in 1982. Security analysts projected a 70 percent drop in normal fourth quarter earnings. In 1983, Tylenol had been predicted to generate half a billion dollars in sales. After the tragedy, analysts predicted that J&J would be fortunate if it generated half of that amount.[6]

Because of its swift and decisive actions, J&J quickly became a corporate role model for dealing with major crises. James Burke did not dodge the press, react with anger, or stonewall the issues. J&J's managers faithfully kept a log of press inquiries so they could get back with information when they had it. They responded quickly and effectively to the general public. As a result, they restored confidence both in J&J as a company and in Tylenol as a product, eventually bringing it successfully back to the market. Although Tylenol did not come back to the 37 percent of the market it commanded before the tragedy, it did rebound to 32 percent, still the largest share of the $1.3 billion over-the-counter pain reliever market. Indeed, 32 percent represents a remarkable recovery, given the fact that its share plummeted to 7 percent at the height of the tragedy.

Because of its complete candor, J&J not only established its credibility, but even steadily increased it during the Tylenol crisis. At one point, one of J&J's top executives was asked by the press, "Can you eliminate entirely the possibility that the poisonings were done by someone on the inside?" The executive said that he could eliminate the possibility of onsite poisoning because cyanide was not present in any of J&J's facilities. Later, however, on learning that trace amounts of cyanide were used in one of J&J's facilities to test the quality of its products, he reconvened the press and stated, "I was wrong; we do have small amounts of cyanide in some of our testing labs; however, I can assure you that our cyanide was not responsible for the poisonings." By being absolutely candid with the press—that is, correcting himself by telling the truth when he was "dead wrong"—J&J's credibility throughout the two crises actually increased. Thus, in a 1987 poll, 91 percent of the respondents stated that J&J had "behaved in an admirable way" during the two Tylenol crises.[7]

Still, after a second Tylenol poisoning, it was reluctantly decided to withdraw Tylenol capsules from the market; J&J executives felt that they could not be protected by current technology. The decision was made to produce Tylenol in the form of caplets because they were more likely to reveal whether they had been contaminated.

The withdrawal of Tylenol from market shelves and the conversion from capsules to caplets are reputed to have cost J&J nearly half a billion dollars. To put it mildly, few organizations can readily absorb such amounts.

The poisoning of Tylenol was a landmark event. One, it was the first time that a major pharmaceutical product had been poisoned without prior warning. For years, food and pharmaceutical companies had received threats that if they did not meet certain extortion demands, their products would be poisoned. But the Tylenol poisonings were not preceded by any notes; in fact, no one even claimed "credit" for them. Two, the perpetrators were never caught. Three, as previously noted, J&J handled the situation so well that it is still regarded by many in the corporate world as *the standard* for CM. And four, the annual number of tampering incidents has never gone down to pre-Tylenol levels.

The fourth point is especially worth noting. Prior to the Tylenol poisonings, the number of annual threats against food and pharmaceutical companies ranged in the hundreds. After the Tylenol incident, the number jumped to the thousands.

J&J Failed to Learn the Proper Lessons of CM

Ironically, because J&J did so well in handling of the Tylenol crisis, it did not learn the proper lessons of CM, especially as the field developed in later years. J&J's top management stated on more than one occasion that prior to the Tylenol poisonings no special training would have helped them manage the situations better. If anything helped, it was their strong corporate culture, credo, and values, which put customer safety ahead of profits. It was also the quality of their top management.

No one disputes that these qualities are both desirable and essential. Furthermore, no one really disputes that at the time there was nothing more or better that J&J could have done, for the modern field of CM was yet to be invented. However, in today's world, J&J's actions are merely necessary at best. They are far from being sufficient given all that we have learned subsequently.

J&J apparently still believes today that no special skills or training either can be given or need to be given to a team of executives before a crisis. In short, there is no way to prepare for the worst prior to its occurrence. My colleagues and I could not disagree more strongly.[8]

J&J did not understand that "acting responsibly" means more than pulling bottles off of shelves, as important and as admirable as this is. It also means *learning* that effective CM demands new organizational procedures and mechanisms. As we shall see, it demands systematic *and* systemic learning on a number of fronts.

Ironically, because J&J did so well in handling its two major crises, it did not learn the proper lessons of CM.

Because J&J did so well without prior preparation, it did not learn that there is all the difference between *victims* to whom crises *happen* and *villains* who *cause* crises or create a crisis-prone culture. As many organizations have sadly found out, it is not only comparatively easy to handle a situation when one is the victim, but it is also extremely easy to go quickly from being a victim to being a villain. For instance, no one disputes that as a victim, J&J performed extremely well. However, when children died in later years due to overdoses of its medication and when Tylenol was implicated in causing liver damage, J&J no longer acted as an exemplary role model. For this reason, J&J is no longer *the* "role model" for CM.

The eminent teacher and management consultant Peter Drucker has observed wisely that many organizations get into trouble *not* because they are a failure from day one, but because they are an overwhelming success for so long. As a result, they repeat unthinkingly the same actions over and over again, even though the environmental conditions that made their initial actions appropriate no longer apply. Drucker has aptly termed this condition "the failure of success." Sadly, this seems to be the moral of the Tylenol poisonings.

Crisis of the Day: From Tylenol to Swiss Air Flight 100

In the years since the Tylenol crisis, a great deal has been learned about how and why crises happen.[9] Much has also been learned about how to manage the aftermath of crises. Even if it is impossible to prevent all crises, their damage can be minimized and the time required to recover from them can be shortened immensely. However, this is possible *if and only if* an organization has the *right* crisis plans and capabilities in place *before* a crisis occurs. It also needs to practice and constantly train for a wide variety of crises.

Unfortunately, the world has recently witnessed a veritable "explosion" of crises of all kinds. The most notable crises in recent years have become household names: Bhopal (the explosion of a dangerous chemical plant in India with the resultant deaths of thousands of people); the explosion of the Space Shuttle Challenger; Chernobyl (the world's worst nuclear disaster); Exxon Valdez (the spilling of thousands of barrels of oil in one of the most pristine and beautiful parts of the world); glass in Gerber's baby food; five USAir crashes in five years; and on and on.

Hardly a day goes by without a major *human*-caused crisis. Among the most recent are mad cow disease (the widespread contamination of British beef with the resultant destruction of thousands of cattle); the crash of the ValuJet airliner, with the loss of 110 lives in the Florida Everglades; the nationwide contamination of strawberries; the bankruptcy of Orange County; the bombing of a government building and the loss of civilian lives in Oklahoma City; the loss of U.S. servicemen in Saudi Arabia due to terrorism; the death of two passengers on a Delta jet due to the explosion of an engine; the still uncertain cause or causes of the destruction of TWA Flight 800 and the explosion of Swiss Air Flight 100; and the tragic destruction of Egypt Air Flight 990 and Alaska Air Flight 261.

It is literally crisis *du jour,* or the "crisis of the day." A major crisis can happen anywhere, anytime, to anyone.

Our Machines Have Mutated into Complex Systems

The quote at the front of this chapter provides an important clue. We have created machines that are now so big and so complicated that they have mutated into entirely new forms.

They are no longer machines. They have become extremely complex, highly intertwined systems.

> *It is literally crisis* du jour. *A major crisis can happen anywhere anytime to anyone.*

These transformed machines or systems have grown so big and so complex that no one, including their designers, fully understands how they will act even in "known" operating conditions. This understanding is even less with regard to how they will react in unforeseen conditions. In effect, we have created "complex systems" that are unmanageable precisely because they have unforeseen, and even worse, unknowable side effects.

In contrast to a simple machine, a system cannot be broken down into its fundamental atoms or components. The separate parts of a system neither exist nor function in isolation from one another. For instance, one cannot take the heart or the lungs out of a human being and still have a live person. Neither the person nor his or her organs can function completely on their own without considerable assistance. Even more to the point, we are just beginning to learn that any one of the individual organs or subsystems of a person affect the total well-being of that individual. In many senses, the mind of a person is not located entirely in the brain, but instead, it is "distributed throughout the entire body" of a person.

The same thing is now true of all of the complex systems that govern and constitute modern societies. For instance, the quote at the front of this chapter shows that the electrical grid is now so complex and intertwined that the most random and seemingly "small events," such as the falling of a single branch on a power line, can disrupt an entire complex system in countless and unforeseen ways. In short, the larger the system, the harder it is to fully understand and to anticipate all of the innumerable, small side effects that can render it inoperable. The larger, the more complex the system, the more vulnerable it is to widespread disruption by even the tiniest and the most isolated of events.

Barely some sixty years ago, a Tylenol poisoning on a nationwide scale would not have been possible. We certainly would not have had to recall an entire nationwide distribution of a product. For one, a single individual could not have gotten on a plane and potentially visited five separate cities in a single day. For another, one could not have coordinated via telephone the activities of a criminal band spread out over the country.

Consider another example. Some sixty years ago, human-caused crises, such as a mine disaster or an explosion, would have mainly affected the particular community in which they occurred. They would not have affected broad, outlying regions. Back then, human disasters were largely confined in space (geography) and time.

For the first time, human-caused crises now rival natural disasters in scope and magnitude.

Today, the situation is vastly different. Humans can affect vast regions of the earth's surface (e.g., through widespread pollution and contamination) and even the earth's atmosphere (e.g., through ozone depletion). We even possess the capability of blowing up the entire planet. Never before has this occurred in human history. For the first time, human-caused crises now rival natural disasters in scope and magnitude.

All of this is due primarily to five major factors that are characteristic of today's world:

1. Complexity
2. Coupling

3. Scope and size
4. Speed
5. Visibility

Complexity refers to the fact that the systems (technological, financial, communication, educational, entertainment, etc.) that we have built have more parts and do more things (calculations, operations, control processes, etc.) than ever before. *Coupling* refers to the fact that everything everywhere can be almost instantaneously connected with and affected by everything anywhere else in the world. *Scope and size* refer to the fact that not only are the systems that we have built bigger in their scope and size, but they are distributed over larger portions of the earth's surface than ever before. As a result, they are larger in their effects on the environment and on humans. *Speed* refers to the fact that both the good and the bad effects of our systems spread themselves more rapidly than ever before. And finally, *visibility* refers to the fact that it is increasingly more difficult, if not outright impossible, to hide the effects of disasters or large-scale systems breakdowns.

The sixty-four trillion dollar question is, "How does one manage in such a world?"

Strategy List for Chapter Two

- Assume responsibility for your products.
- Develop new procedures and mechanisms for systematic and systemic learning.
- Understand that there is a difference between victims to whom crises happen and villains who cause crises or create a crisis-prone environment.
- Avoid relying only on the same success techniques that

have worked in the past, but rather concentrate on constantly developing new techniques.

- Examine the five major characteristics of modern society in relation to your company to help develop safety plans.

Chapter Three

A Best Practice Model

A General Framework for Crisis Management

> "The only way to make bedrock, large-scale change in an organization is to teach it how to *be* different, not how to *do* something differently."
>
> Jac Fitz-enz, *The ROI of Human Capital*

One of the most important findings from studying a large number and a wide variety of different crises is that there *is* a method, or a general framework, for managing major crises. If there weren't such a method or framework, the situation would be truly hopeless. This is not to say that even with the best methods or frameworks one can prevent all crises. Indeed, complete prevention is impossible. Nonetheless, with appropriate and advanced planning and preparation, one can limit substantially both the duration of and the damage caused by major crises. In fact, it has been found repeatedly that those organizations that are prepared for major crises not only recover substantially faster but with significantly less damage than those organizations that are not prepared.[1]

There are other substantial benefits that accrue from being prepared for major crises. One, an organization's major business objectives are less likely to be derailed. For this reason, one is better able to make a strong case for top management giving their strong support for a major program in crisis management. Two, since there are a number of key overlaps between CM and other important organizational programs—

such as environmentalism, issues management, reengineering, strategic planning, and quality assurance—CM can help to effect the integration that is needed between various key programs. Especially in today's world, one cannot keep adding new and costly programs to an organization, no matter how important each individual program is. In today's world, one must take advantage of every possible synergy. For this reason, CM must not be viewed as another separate, stand-alone program. Indeed, unless CM is integrated with other important programs, it will not succeed, and neither will the other programs.

CM must not be viewed as another, stand-alone program. Unless it is integrated with other important programs, it will not succeed, and neither will the other programs.

A Best Practice Model

Exhibit 3-1 shows the components of a Best Practice Model for CM. The five factors—types/risks, mechanisms, systems, stakeholders, and scenarios—are the key elements of the model that must be managed before, during, and after a major crisis.

Before discussing the model in detail, it is especially important to emphasize that *no current organization of which I am aware does well on every one of the key factors*. The model is thus a composite of best practices drawn from a wide variety of organizations. In this sense, the model is an ideal. However, it is not utopian, and there is no reason in principle why every organization cannot do well on each of the factors. In this sense, one of the main purposes of the model is to serve as

Exhibit 3-1: The Components of a Best Practice Model for CM

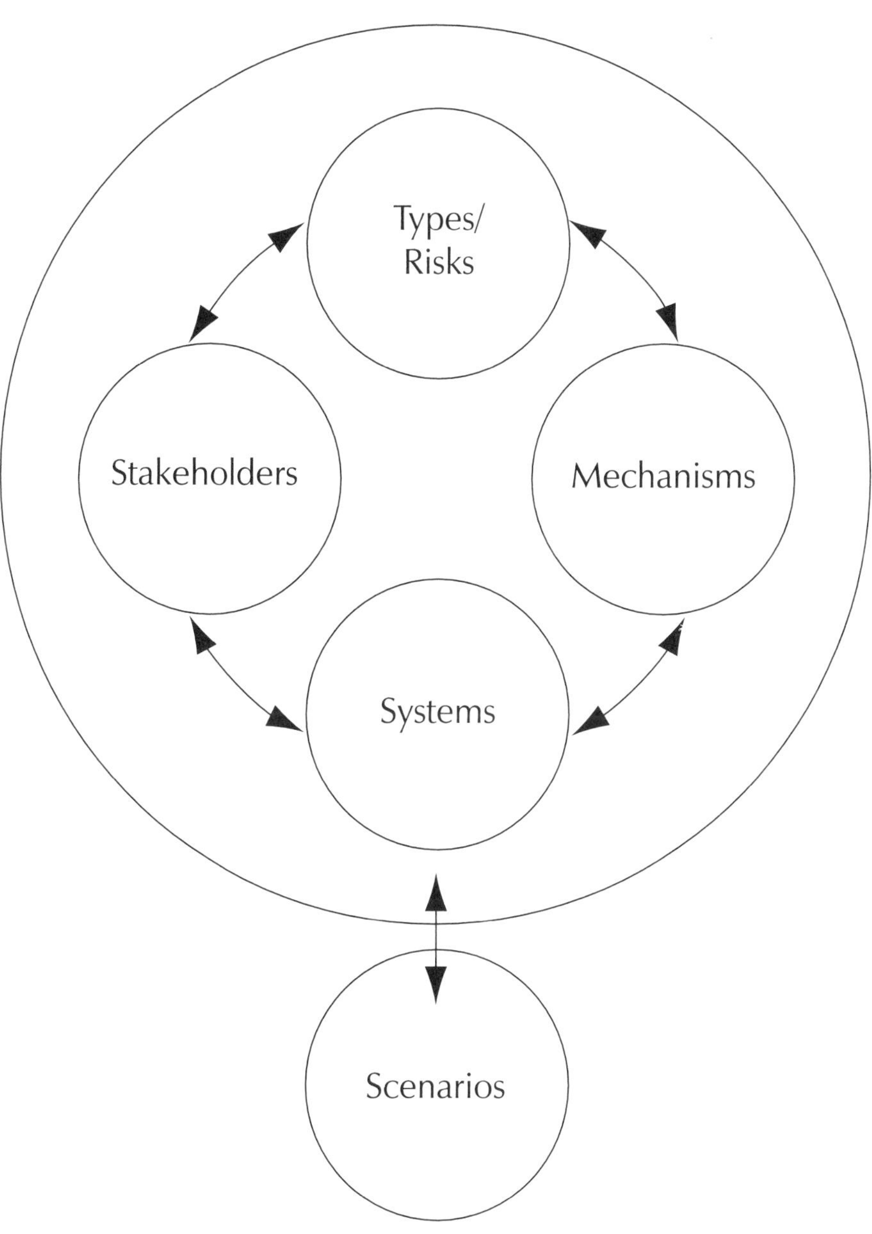

a benchmark against which all organizations should measure their current CM performance.

Types and Risks of Major Crises

Research demonstrates that crises can be sorted into the general categories, families, or types shown in Exhibit 3-2.[2] These are the major types of crises or major risk categories that all organizations should be prepared for. Indeed, a robust "crisis portfolio" consists precisely of the preparation for at least one crisis in each of the various types or families shown in Exhibit 3-2.

Within each general family, specific crises share strong similarities. On the other hand, there are sharp differences between the general categories, families, or types of major crises.

Research in CM also reveals how the best organizations plan for major crises. The first finding is that they attempt to prepare for *at least one* crisis in each of the families.

This finding is especially important for the following six reasons:

◆ First, most organizations only consider at most one or two families. For instance, most organizations prepare at least for natural disasters, such as fires, earthquakes, or floods. Natural disasters occur with great regularity, and they strike all organizations equally. Thus, they are the least threatening to the "collective ego" of organizations. For instance, earthquakes affect all organizations in the Los Angeles area equally. Furthermore, since one can neither predict nor prevent earthquakes, there is not the blame associated with earthquakes as there is with other types of crises—such as workplace violence—that call for special human vigilance and mitigation.

However, even earthquakes have some degree of human blame or responsibility associated with them. For instance, even though we can neither predict nor prevent earthquakes, humans are still charged with the responsibility of designing appropriate buildings that will withstand their worst effects. Humans are also charged with designing appropriate recovery efforts for the victims of earthquakes.

Thus, even those crises that are due solely to "acts of nature" still have a strong human component associated with them, as recent tragedies in Turkey and Venezuela demonstrate so vividly. In the case of Turkey, the failure to design appropriate apartment structures led not only to their collapse but to the deaths of hundreds of occupants. Thus, while Mother Nature may produce earthquakes, humans contribute to their worst effects through shoddy, irresponsible, and even criminal actions.

◆ Two, organizations that do broaden their preparations for crises other than natural disasters most often do it only for "core or normal" disasters that are specific to their particular industry. For instance, no one really has to prod the chemical industry to prepare for explosions and fires, since such occurrences are part of the industry's day-to-day operating experience. Such occurrences are considered a natural part of the territory. For another, no one really has to prod fast food companies to prepare for food contamination and poisoning, since such incidents are also unfortunately part of their day-to-day operating experience.

◆ Three, one does have to continually prod organizations to consider the occurrence of crises from any and all of the families in Exhibit 3-2 simultaneously. That is, major crises occur not only because of what an organization knows, antici-

Exhibit 3-2: Major Crisis Types/Risks

Economic	*Informational*	*Physical (loss of key plants and facilities)*
Labor strikes	Loss of proprietary and confidential information	Loss of key equipment, plants, and material supplies
Labor unrest		
Labor shortage	False information	Breakdowns of key equipment, plants, etc.
Major decline in stock price and fluctations	Tampering with computer records	
		Loss of key facilities
Market crash	Loss of key computer information with regard to customers, suppliers, etc. (Y2K)	Major plant disruptions
Decline in major earnings		

pates, and plans for, but just as much because of what it does not know and does not anticipate. Organizations also need to consider that even when they have prepared for a particular type of crisis and a specific form of it, major crises will still occur because of constantly emerging new environmental factors that give a new wrinkle to old forms.

At this point, it is important to say a few words about the definition of a crisis. Up to this point, I have deliberately avoided defining a crisis, for while they are important, definitions are only really important with regard to the purpose they serve. Unfortunately, it is not possible to give a precise and general definition of a crisis any more than it is possible to predict with exact certainty how a crisis will occur, when it will occur, and why.

Nonetheless, a "guiding definition" is that a crisis is an event that affects or has the potential to affect the *whole* of an organization. Thus, if something affects only a small, isolated

Human Resource	*Reputational*	*Psychopathic Acts*	*Natural Disasters*
Loss of key executives	Slander	Product tampering	Earthquake
Loss of key personnel	Gossip	Kidnapping	Fire
Rise in absenteeism	Sick jokes	Hostage taking	Floods
Rise in vandalism and accidents	Rumors	Terrorism	Explosions
Workplace violence	Damage to corporate reputation	Workplace violence	Typhoons
	Tampering with corporate logos		Hurricanes

part of an organization, it may not be a major crisis. In order for a major crisis to occur, it must exact a *major toll* on human lives, property, financial earnings, the reputation, and the general health and well-being of an organization. More often than not, these occur simultaneously. That is, a major crisis is something that "cannot be completely contained within the walls of an organization." Although they are rare, a few crises, such as the one at Barron's Bank a few years ago, have the potential to destroy a whole organization. And, as the recent experience of the Los Angeles

Major crises occur not only because of what an organization knows, anticipates, and plans for, but just as much because of what it does not know and does not anticipate.

Police Department shows, a major crisis can exact a tremendous financial cost potentially in the billions of dollars.

◆ Four, every organization should plan for the occurrence of *at least one crisis* in each of the various families or types for the reason that *each type can happen to any organization*. For this reason, all of the various types must be considered explicitly.

For instance, consider product tampering. Product tampering does not apply only to food or pharmaceutical organizations. All organizations are vulnerable to a *form* of product tampering that applies specifically to them. For instance, computers are an integral part of every organization. As a result, the true value of computers is neither their hardware nor their software. Rather, it is the information that they contain about customers and other key stakeholders. For instance, a person or persons gaining access to and tampering with an organization's key records could seriously affect that organization's products and services.

Every organization should plan for the occurrence of at least one crisis *in each of the various families or types for the reason that* each type can happen to any organization.

An interesting example is the famous French manufacturer of encyclopedias, Larousse. Apparently, the French are avid collectors and eaters of mushrooms. At particular times of the year, they literally go into the forest with their Larousse encyclopedias at their side. In one section of the encyclopedia there are two facing pages. One side has pictures of the mushrooms that are safe to eat, and the other side has pictures of the unsafe mushrooms. For some unknown reason, whether intentional or not, the labels on the two pages in one edition were reversed. Thus, the safe mushrooms were labeled unsafe, and vice versa. This is a prominent example of *product tampering*. The moral should be absolutely clear: One ignores all or any major types of crises at one's peril!

◆ Five, one fortunately does not have to prepare for every specific type of crisis within each of the families. If this were required, then the task of CM would be rendered both impossible and hopeless. Instead, it has been found that, within limits, it is acceptable to merely prepare for the occurrence of *at least one* type within each of the families. The reasoning behind this is as follows: If no crisis ever happens precisely as one plans for it, then the critical factor is doing one's best to think about the unthinkable prior to its occurrence. Indeed, it has been found that just thinking about the unthinkable prior to its occurrence makes one much more able to think on one's feet and hence to recover from a crisis once it has occurred. The fact that one has anticipated the unthinkable means that one is not paralyzed when it occurs.

If each of the specific types of crises within a particular family share strong similarities, then all that really matters is that one has given serious consideration to each of the families and not necessarily to the particular members within each family. This is not to say that over time one should not attempt to prepare for a broader and wider range of crises, both within and across the families. It merely means that to start on the difficult and onerous road of CM preparation, one need not prepare for everything simultaneously, which is both an impossible and hopeless task.

One of the reasons why I am extremely critical of traditional risk analysis, and as a result, counsel against it, is that it mainly selects only those crises that one has already experienced in the past or with which is familiar. Traditional risk analyses mainly lead one to construct models of the probability of occurrence of various risks. These probabilities are based on historical data of the occurrence of past crises or on various analytical models. The models traditionally give high weight or high ranking to certain types of crises to prepare for, and conversely, low weight or low probability to others. The fallacy behind this procedure is that it is precisely those crises that have not yet occurred to an organization that need to be considered.

The fact that one has anticipated the unthinkable means that one is not paralyzed when it occurs.

In effect, one is caught in a vicious loop. One does not prepare for something until it has happened, and then it may be too late for the organization to recover from the particular crisis. That is, the crises that an organization is not prepared for have the potential to destroy an organization. Thus, the strategy of spreading one's risk across all of the families attempts to correct for this limited oversight.

- Six, another important reason for preparing for at least one crisis in each of the families is that in today's world any crisis is capable of setting off any other crisis and in turn being caused by it. That is, every crisis is capable of being both the cause and the effect of any other crisis. For this reason, the best organizations not only prepare for each individual crisis that they have selected as part of their crisis portfolio, but they also attempt to prepare for the simultaneous occurrence of multiple crises.

Organizations that are prepared for crises have done so by studying past crises and looking for patterns and interconnections between them. They have generated visual maps to better understand how crises unfold over time and how they reverberate both within and beyond the organization.

Again, it is not enough to be prepared for individual crisis in isolation. In today's world no crisis ever happens in isolation. For this reason, one's CM preparations are not effective if one does not consider the impact of every crisis in an organization's crisis portfolio on every other crisis.

In short, CM is strongly systemic. Like total quality management or environmentalism, if CM is not done systemically, then it is not being done well.

When my colleagues and I perform a crisis audit of an organization, one of the things we especially look for is the range and scope of the crises that are prepared for as well as of those crises that are not prepared for. To do this, we deliberately do not give people a copy of Exhibit 3-2. To do so would alert them to the broad range of different types of crises. Instead, we deliberately ask the open-ended question, "What would you consider to be a crisis for your organization?" We then ask them what crises they believe their organization is prepared for and why, and what crises their organization is not prepared for and why. In addition, we ask such questions as what they think their organization will do well in the heat of a crisis, and what it will not do well.

Like total quality management or environmentalism, if CM is not done systemically, then it is not being done well.

In this way, we are able to obtain their informal and implicit "maps" of Exhibit 3-2. That is, we are able to obtain a portrait of the crises that their organization even considers, let alone those it is adequately prepared to handle. In addition, by interviewing an appropriate number of individuals, we are also able to see the similarities as well as the gaps that exist in the thinking of the organization with regard to types of crises.

Mechanisms

One of the other findings of CM research[3] is that there are a relatively small number of mechanisms that are extremely important in planning for and responding to major crises *before, during, and after* their occurrence. Indeed, the fact that these mechanisms apply before, during, and after a major crisis shows why effective CM is *not* merely a case of responding or reacting to a major crisis after it has occurred.

Most serious students and workers in the field of CM acknowledge that the best form of CM is preparation for a major crisis before it has occurred. For this reason, those of us who work and do research in the field of CM know that it is not CM plans per se that are important in preparing for a major crisis. Rather, it is an organization's CM *capabilities* that are all important.

Well in advance of their occurrence, all crises send out a trail of early warning signals.

The various CM mechanisms are for anticipating, sensing, reacting to, containing, learning from, and redesigning effective organizational procedures for handling major crises. Like total quality management or environmentalism, if CM is not done systemically, then it is not being done well. Far in advance of their actual occurrence, all crises send out a trail of early warning signals. If these signals can be picked up and acted upon prior to the occurrence of a crisis, then a crisis can be prevented before it occurs, which is the best possible form of CM. Since we will talk about "signal detection" in Chapter 6, we simply mention its existence and importance at this point. The key point is that signal detection mechanisms have to be in place and operable long before a crisis occurs or they will not function in the heat of an actual crisis. Furthermore, without the proper signal-detection mechanisms, an organization not only makes a major crisis more likely, but it also reduces its chances to bring it under control. Because crises can expand quickly, early signal detection is vital. In addition, one has to have an appropriate range of signal detection mechanisms, since a signal detector for one type of crisis in Exhibit 3-2 will not necessarily be appropriate for the other types.

Even with the best of signal detection mechanisms and programs, crises are inevitable. For this reason, one of the most important aspects of CM is *damage containment*. As its name implies, the purpose of damage containment is to keep the unwanted effects of a crisis from spreading and hence affecting uncontaminated parts of an organization. For instance, damage containment mechanisms are common in the oil industry. Although they are not perfectly effective, especially given the size and the nature of a particular oil spill, the appropriate mechanisms are nonetheless under constant redesign and improvement to keep spills from spreading. As in the case of signal detection, damage containment mechanisms for one type of crisis will not necessarily be appropriate or effective in containing others. Thus, a systematic and systemic program of CM tries as much as is humanly possible to ensure that a variety of damage containment mechanisms is in place and is constantly maintained.

> *Except in cases of criminal malfeasance or negligence, blame and fault finding are not to be encouraged. The main emphasis should be on* no-fault learning.

Two of the most important mechanisms reveal why the vast majority of CM programs are not effective. These concern postcrisis learning and the redesign of systems and mechanisms to improve future CM performance. Unfortunately, few organizations conduct postmortems of crises and near misses, and those that either do not perform them correctly or do not implement their findings. The purpose of such sessions is not to assign fault or blame, but rather to examine the key lessons that need to be learned so that future CM performance can be improved. Except in cases of criminal malfeasance or negligence, blame and fault-finding are not to be encouraged. The main emphasis should be on *no-fault learning*. That is, it should be on the key lessons that need to be learned as well as those that have not been learned in the past, and why. The same emphasis has to be placed on the redesign of systems so that the effects, if not the probabilities, of future crises can be lessened.

Systems

Exhibit 3-3 shows the various systems that govern most organizations. The five components that are key in understanding any complex organization are:

1. Technology
2. Organizational structure
3. Human factors
4. Culture
5. Top management psychology

Exhibit 3-3 is known as the "onion model" of CM.[4] As we peel off the layers of an organization and get beneath its surface, the key factors that drive an organization's behavior become exposed.

Exhibit 3-3: The "Onion Model": The "Layers" of an Organization

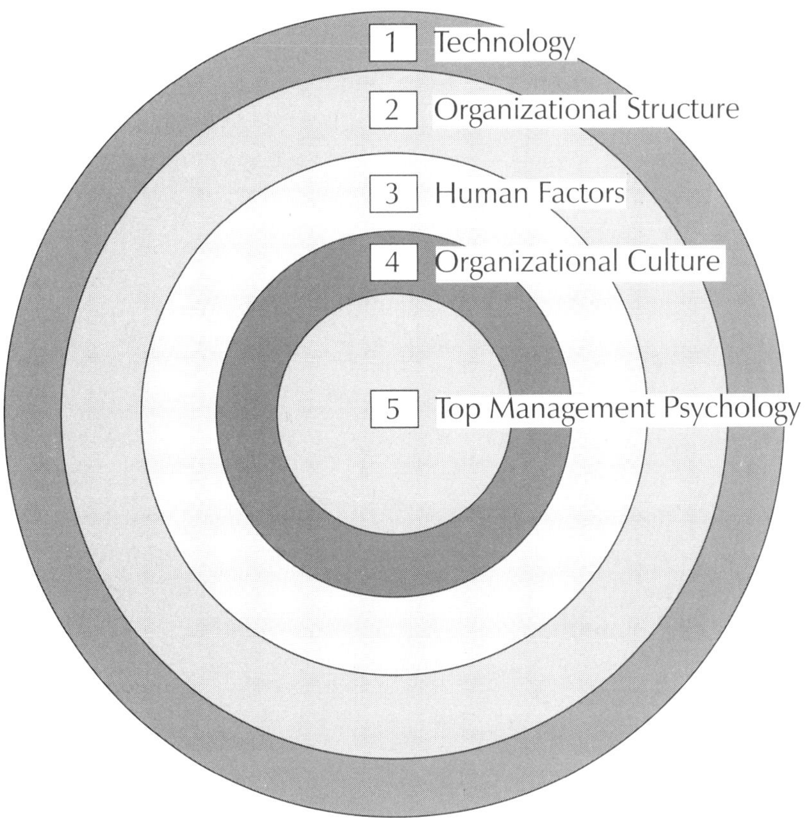

Technology

Let us start with the surface or outer layer of the model. In today's world, all organizations contain complex technologies. These range from computers that process key information to larger plants and processes that manufacture products. Even those organizations in the service area are still involved with complex technologies.

Technology is often the most visible part of an organization, i.e., it can be seen from the highway. Even though most of us may not understand the intricate details of a chemical processing plant, we can at least see the various "protrusions."

The key thing about technology is that it neither exists nor functions in a vacuum. It is run by all-too-human beings, who are error prone. Whether we like it or not, human beings get tired, suffer from stress, or become irritated, all of which contributes to intentional and unintentional errors. The field of "human factors" is precisely that branch of knowledge that exists to assess the causes of human errors and to design systems that, as much as possible, will eliminate or decrease the effects of human errors.

A common example is an airplane cockpit. To the uninitiated, an airplane cockpit is an exercise in extreme chaos at best. The controls are bewildering in themselves. They are laid out in such a fashion that an amateur literally cannot make sense of them, let alone operate them correctly. Yet human factors engineers have created the best possible layout of controls to minimize the chances of catastrophic error for pilots, who often have to operate under stressful conditions. The same considerations are obviously just as critical in the operation of chemical and nuclear power plants.

The next important thing to recognize about technology is that as much as it is run by humans who make errors, it is also embedded in complex organizations that also introduce different sources and kinds of errors. These errors result from the different and multiple layers of an organization across which messages and communications have to travel. They also result from the reward systems that reward certain kinds of behavior and attempt to extinguish other kinds of behavior. All of these factors can both help and hinder the right information reaching the right people in a timely fashion so that the right decisions can be made. For instance, when these factors don't work appropriately, as in the case of Exxon Valdez, then critical time is lost in getting the right people to the scene of a crisis in order to deal with it in a timely and appropriate manner.

Exhibit 3-4 (see page 46) shows the potential interactions between the subsystems of Exhibit 3-3. That is, it shows that the operation of technology is affected by people and the organizations in which it is embedded, etc.

Organizational Structure and Culture

To get at the underlying layers of an organization, and to understand how the various subsystems can interact, one has to be privy to the inner workings of an organization. This requires that we take an even deeper look inside an organization. To do this, we have to examine in detail the policies and procedures that govern an organization's behavior.

The deepest parts of an organization reside in its culture and in the psychology of its top management. These two layers are the most difficult to get at, and for this very reason, the most critical determinants of an organization's CM performance.

Defense Mechanisms

Exhibit 3-5 shows some of the key components of an organization's culture and its relationship to CM. One of the first and most important discoveries regarding CM was the identification and the assessment of organizational culture.[5] It was found that organizations, like individuals, make use of various *defense mechanisms* in order to deny their vulnerabilities to major crises and hence to justify why they did not need to engage in effective CM. The various mechanisms can not only be identified, but are easily sorted and labeled.

Exhibit 3-4: Interactions among the Layers of the Onion Model

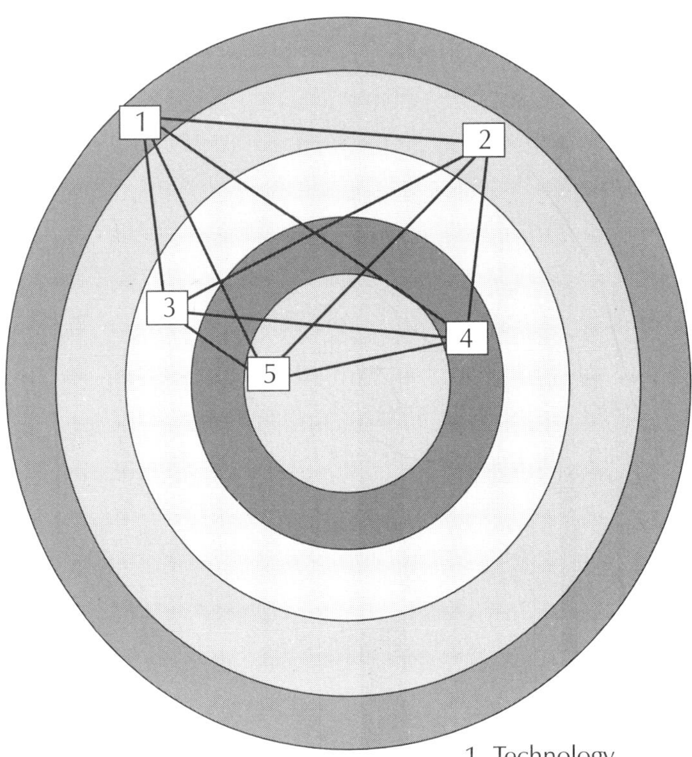

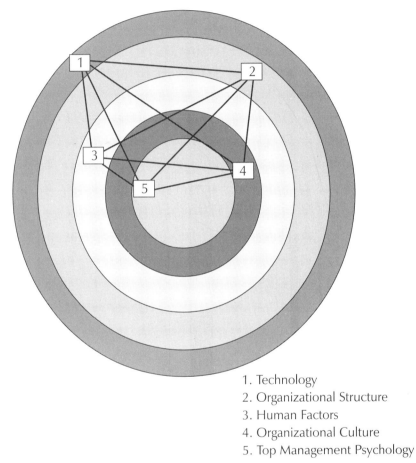

1. Technology
2. Organizational Structure
3. Human Factors
4. Organizational Culture
5. Top Management Psychology

Exhibit 3-5 is merely a small sampling of the wide variety of defense mechanisms that organizations use to deny their vulnerabilities to major crises. What is both interesting and important is that these mechanisms follow almost to the letter the classic Freudian defense mechanisms that apply to individuals.

For instance, the first item in the table is *denial.* This mechanism completely denies an organization's vulnerability

Exhibit 3-5: Organizational Defense Mechanisms

Type of Defense Mechanism	*Interpretation/Example*
Denial	Crises only happen to others. We are invulnerable.
Disavowal	Crises happen, but their impact on our organization is small.
Idealization	Crises do not happen to good organizations.
Grandiosity	We are so big and powerful that we will be protected from crises.
Projection	If a crisis happens, it must be because someone else is bad or out to get us.
Intellectualization	We don't have to worry about crises since the probabilities of their occurring are too small.
	Before a crisis can be taken seriously, one would have to measure precisely its odds of occurrence and its consequences.
Compartmentalization	Crises cannot affect the whole of our organization since the parts are independent of one another.

to crises. Somehow or another, the organization is exempt from a whole class of crises, if not from crises altogether. The next item is the classic Freudian mechanism of *disavowal*. Unlike denial, disavowal recognizes the existence and the threat of a major crisis, but it downplays its importance or seriousness. In other words, disavowal diminishes the size, the magnitude, or the importance of a crisis.

Exhibit 3-5 is important because it can be used to assess both the kinds of defense mechanisms that an organization uses as well as the extent to which they are used. In effect, the mechanisms constitute an organization's culture with regard to CM. For instance, an organization that subscribes to a preponderance of the mechanisms in Exhibit 3-5 almost ensures that it will not take CM seriously. As a consequence, the organization will have dramatically increased its odds that it will experience a major crisis. It also seriously lengthens the time that it will take the organization to recover from a crisis.

Organizations use a variety of defense mechanisms to deny their vulnerability to major crises. These mechanisms follow the classic Freudian defense mechanisms that apply to individuals.

Stakeholders

Stakeholders involve the broad range of internal and external parties who have to cooperate, share crises plans, and participate in the training and the development of organizational capabilities in order to respond to a range of crises. Stakeholders range from internal employees to external, city, community, state, national, and even international parties, such as the Red Cross, police departments, armies, and fire departments, all of whom may be called upon to help in a major crisis. What is key about stakeholders is that important relationships among them have to be worked on years in advance if an organization is to develop the capabilities and the smooth functioning that are required in the heat of a major crisis.

Scenarios

Good scenarios are the "integrative glue" that binds all of the preceding factors together. A good CM scenario is the "best case, worst case'' scenario that one can construct with regard to how a crisis will affect an organization. That is, a good crisis scenario involves the occurrence of a type of crisis that the organization has neither considered nor has prepared for. In addition, the crisis should not only occur at a completely unanticipated time, but at the worst possible time, such as over a holiday weekend. Furthermore, a good scenario involves the breakdown of the most taken-for-granted, well-designed, and well-performing systems. It should include a chain reaction of crises—related or not related—happening all at the same time. In effect, a good crisis scenario is a plan for how the unthinkable can and will occur.

A good CM scenario is the ''best case, worst case'' scenario that one can construct with regard to how a crisis will affect an organization.

Concluding Remarks

All of the preceding factors constitute not only a set of ideal benchmarks by which any organization should evaluate itself, but the scorecard that the media will use to evaluate and to ask questions about an organization's crisis performance. This is precisely why it is important for an organization to undergo crisis training and preparation. In short, it is the reason why an organization has to ask the toughest questions of itself.

No matter how hard an organization is on itself, I can guarantee without qualification that the outside media—one of the most important of all stakeholders—will be even harsher. For this reason, a successful crisis audit of an organization is not only that which points out the most serious weaknesses of the organization, but one that is absolutely and ruthlessly blunt and honest. Although the prime purpose of such an audit is not necessarily to offend people, the report should be so honest as to cause those who prepared it to be fired!

In the end, effective CM comes down to two main questions: "How much reality can an organization bear to learn about itself with regard to its crisis strengths and weaknesses?" and "How much is an organization willing to invest to correct its weaknesses and improve upon its strengths?"

Strategy List for Chapter Three

- Integrate crisis management with other programs; do not make it a separate program.
- Create a crisis portfolio that prepares the company for at least one crisis in each of the seven categories: economic, informational, physical, human resources, reputational, psychopathic acts, and natural disasters.
- Don't limit the crisis portfolio to just natural disasters or to disasters specific to your industry.
- Don't rely on traditional risk analysis, which concentrates only on those crises that have occurred in the past.
- Manage the five factors involved in a crisis: stakeholders, mechanisms, types/risks, systems, and scenarios.
- Look for patterns and interconnections in past crises.
- Generate maps to understand how a crisis develops and reverberates within and outside of the organization.
- Consider the impact that one crisis will have on the other seven categories of crises. Will it generate new crises?

- Set up mechanisms to detect the early warning signs of a crisis.
- Set up damage containment mechanisms.
- Conduct postmortems of crises and near misses.
- Avoid using such meetings as a means to assign blame but rather concentrate on improving signal detection and crisis prevention.
- Examine the five systems that govern an organization: technology, organizational structure, human factors, culture, and top management psychology.
- Determine how crises can develop from these systems, and how you can reduce errors.
- Identify the defense mechanisms the company uses to promote denial that crises can happen to them.

Chapter Four

Should We Tell the Truth?

The Varieties of Truth and Telling the Truth

". . . salacious tales of sex, murder, and corruption date back to the founding of the republic. What *is* [Getlin's emphasis] new, however, are the *scope* and *intensity* [emphasis added] of these media spectacles. America has entered what some observers are calling an Age of Permanent Scandal—an era when marathon stories like Clinton-Lewinsky and the Simpson murder are beamed into homes twenty-four hours a day, for months and even years at a time.

". . . Scandal, with apologies to Karl Marx, may be the opiate of the people.

"[As Michael Kinsley put it:] 'It began with the Gulf War, because fifteen minutes after it was over, nobody remembered it,' he said. 'The war begat O.J., and O.J. begat Monica. These stories create an adrenaline rush that wears off—and we're all addicted. We need another fix.' "

Josh Getlin, "Suffering Scandal Fatigue"
Los Angeles Times[1]

The task of CM would be relatively easy if the general framework that was presented in the previous chapter was all that one needed to manage major crises effectively. Unfortunately, this is far from the case. As the preface to this book indicated, questions of individual and organizational character are paramount. For this reason, a general framework for CM, while necessary, is not sufficient. In addition, one must confront questions of character at both the individual and the organizational level.

Telling the Truth

Even a cursory review of the Tylenol crisis presented in Chapter Two shows that telling the truth played a major role in its handling. Indeed, telling the truth plays a major role in all crises. Consider, for instance, the following three potential, if not actual, crisis situations.

Episode One

In opposition to nearly all of her basic values, and over her strong objections, a young woman is being heavily pressured by her boss to design a Web site that is highly offensive to her and to her coworkers. A high-paying client has commissioned the firm to design a Web site featuring lewd and degrading images of women. Although her boss does not like the project, given the firm's extremely precarious financial situation, he feels that he has no choice but to accept it. (Even though the young woman believes strongly in "free speech," this is not enough to persuade *her* that *she* is *the one* in particular who needs to defend it in this particular instance. The guarantee of free speech does not compel a private person or party to enact it in every case. It merely means that the government shall make or pass no laws restricting free speech. What a particular person or private company does is part of their management policy, not an edict of government.)

Episode Two

The loan committee of a major U.S. bank, made up of its top executives, is conducting its monthly review of major loan applications. One in particular is especially promising. All of the numbers and financial analyses indicate that it promises to deliver extremely high rates of return at an exceptionally low risk. The committee is therefore strongly predisposed to grant the loan. At literally the eleventh hour, one of the committee members asks casually, "By the way, what is the business?" Someone digs through a thick pile of papers, and after what seems like an eternity, announces with noticeable distress in his voice, "Oh my God, it's pornography!"

Episode Three

Charges of impeachment against a sitting U.S. President are successfully voted out of the U.S. House of Representatives for only the second time in American history. The President is charged with lying under oath with regard to an illicit sexual affair with a White House intern half his age. The sordid details are made public by the office of the independent prosecutor a few short months after the President went on television, stared directly into the cameras, and stated angrily, "I did not have sex with that woman!" Later, he is forced to admit that he did indeed have sex with "that woman." His admission fails to satisfy the political opposition, who successfully vote through charges of impeachment, even though they eventually fail to garner the required votes in the U.S. Senate to force the President's eventual removal from office. Nonetheless, the Office of the President is seriously tarnished, along with nearly all of the institutions involved, including the Congress, the Office of the Independent Prosecutor, and the news media.

Individual members of Congress are also forced to resign after Larry Flynt, publisher of the pornographic magazine *Hustler,* reveals sordid details about their past. As a result, more than one political commentator makes the shrewd and wry observation that, "For all practical purposes, Larry Flynt and *Hustler* are running the country, i.e., setting the political agenda!"

What Do These Three Episodes Have in Common?

Besides illicit sex, which for sizable numbers of Americans is apparently no longer a sin, what do these three episodes have in common? They span the spectrum of situations in which telling, or not telling, the truth plays a major role.

The first episode involves the *potential commission* of an act for which the chances are almost virtually certain that it will lead to the *compromise* or the *eventual distortion* of the truth. The first episode thus involves a person being strongly pressured to do something for which she will undoubtedly later be greatly embarrassed. It is also highly likely that the person doing the pressuring will also be embarrassed, and hence, will engage in a further distortion of the truth.

The second episode involves the case where a group of senior executives *are actually deciding* whether to do something that is almost guaranteed to turn into something highly embarrassing both to them and to their institution. The third episode involves a situation where an individual *has already committed* an embarrassing act, and furthermore, *has already lied* about it.

At some point in our lives all of us will face compromising situations. They most likely will involve not simply "telling the truth" but "sticking up for one's basic values" under the most difficult and trying situations.

Although obviously very few of us will ever be top executives of a bank or a major institution, let alone President of the United States, at some point in our lives all of us will face compromising situations. Although these situations will differ from the three opening episodes, they most likely will involve not simply "telling the truth" but "sticking up for one's basic values" under the most difficult and trying of situations. Even though the particular circumstances of each episode are different, each has the potential to cause significant and long-lasting damage to the individual's personal reputation, to stain their character indelibly, as well as cause irreparable harm to their institutions.

In the first episode the potential for self-deception—in effect, lying to oneself—is especially high. This is particularly the case where one has convinced oneself that "there are no other choices or alternatives that are available.'' This is not only potentially true of the young woman's boss, but even of the young woman herself. This is also the case with the young woman's colleagues, since the pressure to go along with the group, to be a ''team player,'' is always great, especially in times of financial distress.

In effect, the young woman is being pressured to lie to herself, and by doing so, to go directly against some of her most basic values. The situation is made even more difficult by the fact that in general she likes her job, her colleagues, and even her boss. In addition, this was the very first time that she had ever been asked to do something inappropriate.

It was only after repeatedly saying ''No!'' to her boss and being threatened with the loss of her job that she finally hit upon a viable course of action. She said that she would produce the Web site, but only under one condition. Upon its completion, she would show the site to her boss's daughter, his wife, and his mother. The boss's reaction was instantaneous. The contract was canceled immediately, and the whole incident was never mentioned again.

In the case of the bank, upon learning that the exact nature of the business was ''legal'' pornography (it did not involve the sexual exploitation of children or acts of violence against women), one of the senior officers asked *the* central, and hence, damning question, ''Do we want to be known as the Porn Bank? Surely not!'' This one question was enough to completely outweigh all of the projected profits. In effect, the consideration became as follows: ''How does it profit a bank if it makes all the money in the world but in the process loses its most precious thing, its venerable reputation and character? Similarly, what profit will the executives of the bank have if in the process they lose their most prized and privileged possession as well? How much money does it take to sell one's reputation and soul?''

The third episode is potentially the most interesting as well as the most important of all. This is not merely because it involves the President of the United States—although undeniably this is a strong factor—but rather because over the course of our lives, everyone is guaranteed to do at least one thing that if it were to come to light, its revelation would cause severe humiliation, guilt, and shame.

There is also another consideration that makes the third episode or situation especially pertinent in today's world. It shows how far we are from truly learning the critical lessons of CM.

What Crisis Management Has to Teach

As I pointed out in Chapters One and Two, CM is the study of why *human*-caused crises occur, and what, if anything, can be done to prevent them, or keep them from becoming worse once they have occurred. Unlike natural disasters, human-caused crises, such as Bhopal, Chernobyl, Exxon Valdez, Mad Cow Disease, or the bribery scandals that have rocked the International Olympic Committee, do not need to happen. They are neither inevitable nor ordained.

In contrast with natural disasters over which we often have little control, human-caused crises result because of improper human actions or inactions. Thus, in principle, they are preventable. For this very reason, the public is often rightly outraged when they occur. True, we can be outraged against Mother Nature for the occurrence of an earthquake or a typhoon, but it is not the same kind of rage we feel when, say, contemplating the tragic explosion of the space shuttle Challenger and the resulting loss of seven lives.

Information technologies, such as e-mail, television, and the news media, play a significant part in the occurrence of major crises, as well as in their subsequent management. Public exposure for so-called private behavior can create a megacrisis. However, information technologies are also responsible for something far more significant.

Modern information technologies have radically altered the basic nature of privacy and secrecy in modern societies.[2] As a result, they have rewritten one of the fundamental, underlying rules of society. In a word, because of the explosive growth of information technologies and their intrusion into every nook and cranny of our lives, in effect, *there are no secrets anymore—none, period*!

Because of the explosive growth of information technologies and their intrusion into every nook and cranny of our lives, in effect, there are no secrets anymore—none, period!

Technology in general, and television in particular, have altered our lives profoundly in ways we are just beginning to comprehend.[3] Technology has invaded the once "back-stage," private lives of persons and institutions to such a degree that, for all practical purposes, everything is now "up front and personal" for all the world to see. As a result, there are no secrets in the strict sense anymore because there are no hard, firm boundaries anymore between public and private acts or spaces.

For instance, consider the case of Rodney King, the motorist whose severe beating by the Los Angeles police was captured on tape and then subsequently played over and over again on television worldwide. One of the most important aspects of this particular case has received virtually no attention: The widespread use of camcorders by ordinary citizens has turned everyone into potential investigative reporters! The invention and distribution of camcorders has not only allowed people to record pictures of their personal friends and families, but it has also allowed them to record events once open only to professional photographers, news reporters, or documentary film makers. Thus, how the police once behaved "backstage" in the relative comfort, security, and privacy (i.e., bounded, secluded space) of the station house, or on isolated streets, is no longer exempt from widespread public scrutiny. Backstage events (private space) have now become front-stage revelations. Indeed, they are now the subject of prime-time news shows around the world.

Today, the world is so interconnected in space and time that any event around the globe can potentially affect other events in ways of which we are only dimly aware.

Peter Schwartz, president of the Global Business Network, has pointed out that human-rights organizations are even distributing free video cameras to the citizens in countries with poor records of human-rights violations so that they can film the incriminating acts by their governments and send them directly to CNN![4]

If an event is dramatic enough, then it can become news anywhere and at any time. In addition, events that happen anywhere can affect other seemingly unrelated events anywhere in the world. Chernobyl is a perfect example. It took approximately two weeks for the nuclear cloud of radiation from Chernobyl to encircle the globe and physically contaminate salmon off the coast of the state of Washington. However, it took less than half a day for the grain markets in Chicago to react sharply to the catastrophe. If the breadbasket of the former Soviet Union was knocked out of commission for a hundred years due to the dangerous radiation released by Chernobyl, then the market for future grain prices in Chicago was affected dramatically. The end result is that "business time and space" are now free from the moorings of "physical time and space."

Today, the world is so interconnected in space and time that any event around the globe can potentially affect other events in ways of which we are only dimly aware. In light of this fundamental alteration of ordinary space and time, as well as the sheer uncertainty of knowing which improbable events out of thousands will connect to affect our lives, organizations, and world, how do we manage institutions?

Some thirty years ago, Alvin Toffler astutely observed that we were suffering from "future shock," a phrase he introduced into the language.[5] Essentially, future shock is the growing inability to function normally because of the rapid speedup and highly stressful overload of events. What Toffler did not foresee, and is thus still unable to explain even in his most recent book, *Power Shift,* is that future shock is itself being exacerbated by a complementary complicating force, which can be called *Boundary Shock.* As a result, the effects on people that he foresaw are even more intense.

The point of all of this is that in today's world, it is truly the height of folly to believe that what one says and does behind closed doors, or in private settings, will remain there. The constant 24-hours-a-day, 365-days-a-year craving for news—everything everywhere is local news—has created a media monster whose appetite is voracious. What *every* public figure says is potentially Page One news in the *Los Angeles Times, Wall Street Journal, New York Times, or Washington Post,* or a lead story on CNN or the "Six O'clock Action News." It is the height of arrogance and foolishness to think otherwise.

The Johari Window

There is a simple framework that is typically discussed in beginning college courses in group behavior. This framework is extremely helpful in understanding what is so different about today's world. After the first names of its inventors, Joe and Harry, it is known as the Johari Window (see Exhibit 4-1).[6]

The Johari Window says in effect that *it takes at least two people to know any one person fully*. Look at the two rows in Exhibit 4-1. The "Known" row indicates what a person knows about himself or herself. The "Unknown" row indicates what a person does not know or is unaware of about himself or herself. Thus, the "Unknown" row is meant to stand for all of those things that a person is ignorant about, not conscious of, or is unable to see from the vantage point of others.

Next, look at the two vertical columns in the exhibit. The "Known" column indicates what others directly know or can

Exhibit 4-1: The Johari Window

		Another Person	
		Known	**Unknown**
Yourself	**Known**	1. The Public Domain	2. The Hidden Domain
	Unknown	4. The Blind Domain	3. The Mysterious Domain

find out about a person. On the other hand, the "Unknown" column stands for what they do not know about a person or cannot easily find out, if at all.

Now consider the four cells of Exhibit 4-1. Cell 1 stands for the "Public Domain." It represents all those things that you know about yourself and that others know about you as well. It thus represents the case of public or shared information. Cell 2, on the other hand, represents what you know about yourself, but what others do not know. It thus represents the "Hidden Domain." Cell 3 represents all of those things that you, as well as others, do not know. It is rightly called the "Mysterious Domain." Finally, Cell 4 represents what others know about you, but what you do not know about yourself. It is thus aptly called the "Blind Domain."

With the incessant rise of the tabloid media, its intrusion into every nook and cranny of our lives, the veritable explosion of exploitative talk shows where apparently untold numbers of people are willing to shamelessly reveal their darkest secrets, the "hidden" domain has for all practical purposes vanished from modern life. That is to say, the odds are almost one hundred percent that at some point in time the contents of the "hidden" domain will be exposed. If this weren't bad enough, then the constant blare of the media has also greatly increased the odds that the contents of the "mysterious" domain will be ruthlessly exposed as well. Thus, once again, for all practical purposes, the "hidden" side of life has virtually disappeared. Public knowledge of the "mysterious" side has essentially increased to the point where virtually anything of consequence can and will be known about us, especially those in public life.

This raises issues and concerns that have not been present to the same degree ever before in human history. It is now no longer a matter of *whether* the worst, the darkest secrets, will be found out and revealed about a person, but rather *how soon* and under *which circumstances,* and finally, *who* will reveal them. If this is indeed the new order of things, then the question becomes, "At the first hint that the worst will be exposed about you, how much, if anything, should you say or reveal about yourself?" Notice that it is no longer a matter of whether you *will* tell the worst and the "whole truth" about yourself, but only *when* and *under what circumstances* you will tell freely or be forced to tell.

It is now no longer a matter of whether *the worst, the darkest secrets, will be found out and revealed about a person, but rather* how soon *and under* which circumstances, *and finally,* who *will reveal them.*

What Ought One to Do?

The question whether one should reveal completely the deepest and darkest truths about oneself is not the kind of question that can be answered with a yes or no, since these are not simple black or white issues. Nonetheless, one can still lay out the general kinds of considerations that everyone is well advised to take into account in fashioning the kind of response that is best suited for the particular circumstances they face.

As an important way of shedding light on the issue of truth telling, I'm going to beg the readers' indulgence and ask them to imagine Niccolo Machiavelli as a Crisis Consultant for today's "Princes" of business. I can hear Machiavelli saying:

Machiavelli: *Don't you realize that the best way to gain the upper hand over your enemies is by controlling the worst about yourself, by releasing it on your terms and thereby becoming "saved again" in the eyes of the public? Don't you realize that the thing that will confound your enemies the most, put them completely off guard, is the very fact that you are willing to reveal the darkest, innermost secrets about your checkered past? Don't you realize that this is exactly the thing that they are most afraid to do about themselves?*

By getting the worst out about yourself, you will have preempted them. You will have also issued a supreme challenge for them to do exactly the same. And if one thing is true about humankind, it is that one does not wish to do anything that is risky or reckless. Therefore, dear Prince, I advise you to act as boldly as possible. I urge you to do the exact opposite of the so-called best advice of your trusted advisors.

I know that what I am advising you now is the exact opposite of what I have counseled you to do in the past. Then, I advised you to gain power and to hold it by whatever means possible. I urged you to act with deceit, cunning, and to employ lying. However, I now realize, and you must too, that these things no longer work in today's world. Now you must confound your enemies with frank and brutal honesty. Trust me. If you do, you will win by different means that are adapted to the spirit of the age.

Remember, dear Prince, what those who have not followed my advice have been forced to do:

> *In the very end, they have been forced to admit and to say the very things that they said they would never do in the beginning, that is, come completely clean! President Clinton! Need I say more?*

In terms of Exhibit 4-2, the position that Machiavelli has been arguing is represented by Cell 2, or the "Preemptive Strike" strategy. However, with a little reflection, one can see that depending on the particular details of a situation, Machiavelli could easily argue for any of the strategies represented by the four cells of Exhibit 4-2. For instance, Machiavelli could argue that if a powerful person *knows* the truth about someone, then sooner or later one will be "forced to tell the truth." Nonetheless, given the good corporate lawyer that he

Exibit 4-2: Telling the Truth

		Another Person**	
		Known	**Unknown**
Yourself*	**Reveal/ Tell**	1. Forced to Tell the Truth	2. Preemptive Strike
	Don't Reveal/ Don't Tell	4. Stonewall It	3. Play the Odds

*The two rows indicate two very different kinds of actions that a person can take.

**The two columns represent whether another person knows or does not know the truth about a first person, or "yourself."

is, Machiavelli would still argue, "Don't reveal/tell the truth about yourself until you are forced to do so. Anything else is extremely foolish."

On the other hand, Machiavelli could also argue that even if someone powerful *knows* the unsavory truth about a person, deny or "stonewall it" as long as possible.

Finally, Machiavelli could even argue the position that as long as those in powerful positions *don't know* the unsavory truth about a person, then one is well advised to "play the odds" in denying the truth.

Depending upon the circumstances, it is possible to employ all of the strategies indicated in Exhibit 4-2. For instance, one could argue that as the Monica Lewinsky scandal unfolded, President Clinton not only played out all of the strategies in the exhibit, but he shifted between them as the circumstances changed. In this particular case, Machiavelli could even claim victory, because by playing the strategy outlined in Cell 4, the President in a very real sense ended up "winning." It could even be argued that President Clinton's accusers ended up losing as much as, if not more than, he did. For this reason, Machiavelli could well contend that he or she who forces another person to tell the unsavory truth had better be prepared to have "equally unsavory truths" revealed about himself or herself!

Since no single crisis advisor is ever likely to cover all the bases, I can also easily imagine three other important historic characters as prominent advisors: Sigmund Freud, Mahatma Ghandi, and William James. Each of these characters captures different considerations in fashioning a response that is appropriate for each individual and the details of their particular situation. At this particular point in the discussion, I can well imagine that our other three "crisis advisors" are no longer able to contain themselves. Indeed, they would probably blurt out almost in unison something as follows:

ALL: *The thing that we find most detestable about your position, Machiavelli, is the unsavory ethical principle that underlies it. Since you rarely state it yourself, we're going to have to extract it ourselves. For instance, take Cell 2 of your Exhibit 4-2 as an illustration. Here is the "grand ethical principle" that underlies your position:*

If and only if no one currently knows the "unsavory truth" about a person, but nonetheless there exists the strong possibility that at least one other *person will "know" it,* then and only then *ought one to tell the "complete and awful truth" about oneself!*

They continue:

ALL: *We are quite well aware that you don't think much of ethics. The only ethics that you do think well of, if you think of it at all, are those notions that are based on considerations of survival and power. But even on your very own terms, your position is precarious. You are advising someone to come clean only because it will supposedly preempt one's adversaries. By doing so, you ignore your own insights regarding the nature of what has changed precisely in today's world. You advise one to enact a preemptive strike when the chances are very high that the truth will be found out. But if this is the case, why then wouldn't people also ultimately find out the strategy that you have recommended, i.e., a "Preemptive Strike"? That is, if there are indeed few, if any, precious secrets left in today's world, then why should your own rea-*

soning regarding what to do in a crisis situation be any less secret?

Isn't your strategy like the Ford Pinto crisis? The executives involved never counted on the fact that their strategy of opting to pay the settlement costs of those killed in a rear-end collision due to the faulty design of the Pinto's gas tank would be found out. They didn't count on the fact that it would become widespread public knowledge that Ford's executives considered it cheaper to pay the insurance costs for the small percentage of lives that would be lost rather than redesigning the car. When the public did find out, then this caused "additional costs" that they had not counted on. In short, you are not calculating the "full costs" of your own strategy.

Our three crises consultants continue:

ALL: *Machiavelli, your recommendations are—you have admitted as much yourself—merely a new form of deception that amounts to deceiving people by telling the truth! However, the fundamental flaw in this reasoning is this: What is to prevent the public from learning of this form of deception? How many cycles of deception do you think you can engage in before you will be found out?*

The worst thing about your strategy, Machiavelli, and why it will really not work, is that it will not stop the underlying dynamics that made a person engage in embarrassing behavior in the first place. Above all, this is why your strategy really is doomed to fail. It fails to treat, and thereby to halt, the underlying disease. Indeed, it merely perpetuates it. In this sense, you are one of the biggest co-conspirators or enablers of dysfunctional processes around!

At this point, our three crisis consultants begin to diverge and to speak in their own separate voices.

Freud: *Machiavelli, you are the one that is naive. You delude yourself, as many do, into believing that one can win merely by exercising conscious, rational thinking, i.e., strategizing. You fail to understand that conscious, rational thinking is only the small tip of the huge iceberg that constitutes the full mind or psyche. To put it differently, rational thinking is often at the "complete mercy" of the strongest unconscious impulses. To put it in crude terms, President Clinton didn't get into trouble because of his brains, but rather, because of his lack of impulse control. I advise telling the truth because it is the only viable means of healing a person's psyche.*

You fail to grasp an essential point about the psyche. There is always *"another person" who "knows" the truth about a person. That "other person" is your unconscious. If you block out completely the message of this internal voice, if you exhibit no guilt whatsoever with regard to your actions, then in effect you are or have become a sociopath, for the only kind of person that can do this successfully is a sociopath.*

You fail to grasp the true meaning of ethics. To be ethical is to do the "right things" and to tell

> *the truth when no one is there to know what one has done* except *the inner voice of one's conscience.*
>
> **Ghandi:** *I advise telling the truth because it is the only means of healing one's soul.*
>
> **William James:** *Your trouble, Machiavelli, is that you substitute simple-minded tables and gimmicks for systemic, i.e., expansive thinking. You truly fail to think "outside of the boxes."*

Our three advisors are adamant and have become quite heated. They almost shout with one voice what they would have advised the President to have done from the very beginning:

> **ALL:** *If we had been advising President Clinton, then early on we would have urged him to say something like the following:*
>
>> *I'm taking the unprecedented action of speaking to you tonight in order to admit that I have a problem. It's akin to alcoholism. As a result, I have decided to seek professional treatment while I am in office.*
>>
>> *Like many senior executives with major corporations who are in treatment for their alcoholism, my problem does not affect my ability to perform my duties effectively. I believe that by seeking treatment I can render one of the greatest legacies to the Presidency.*
>>
>> *No longer can anyone who seeks or serves in*

this office do so without the constant scrutiny that comes with it. In saying this, I am not complaining about the situation. I am merely stating a fact. Therefore, the question is no longer whether any of us is flawed, but whether we honestly acknowledge our flaws and *are willing to work on them. I will not discuss with the public the nature of the treatment I am seeking nor my progress on my problem. I leave it to the American people to judge whether they are willing to have a person who is less than perfect serve them while he or she is willing to undergo treatment.*

ALL: *Of course, in the beginning, we would have had no sure way of knowing whether President Clinton was guilty of sexual misconduct. However, from what we know of his past,*[7] *we wouldn't be surprised if he were because it unfortunately fits the pattern of Adult Children of Alcoholics, or ACOAs.*

ACOAs learn early in life to function in crisis situations because that is *their daily reality. Even worse, they often only feel alive in crisis situations. When life is running smoothly, they feel discomfort for they only know how to function in a crisis. As a result, they unconsciously have to create crises for themselves. Why else would an otherwise intelligent and rational person jeopardize their high position? But that's precisely the point! The inability to control impulses is not solely a matter of rational thinking.*

We have learned painfully in the business arena

that if a person admits to alcoholism and is willing to seek serious treatment, then this is no longer cause for his or her dismissal. If one refuses to admit one has a problem, or to seek treatment, then that is another issue.

Are we now willing to extend the same acceptance and understanding to those who hold the highest office in our land?

Notice carefully that the scenario we have outlined applies whether the President had been forced to resign from office or not. He could still cement his place in history by leaving on a higher note of openness and honesty.

We proclaim as a nation that we constantly want leaders who are straight with us and have high character. But are we willing to accept that high character does not mean one who is free from all defects, but instead has the strength to admit one's defects?

William James: *I have one more comment to make. It is meant to be perfectly outrageous. Are we finally willing to consider replacing the "Office of the Independent Prosecutor" with that of the "Office of the Independent Therapist?"*

Closing Remarks

Although they certainly don't call it by that name, the news media directly employ a variant of the Johari Window. One of the first questions that they invariably raise with regard to any crisis is, "When did you know about the particular situation, and if you knew about it, why didn't you do something about it then? And, if you didn't know about it, why didn't you?" Either way, one is in deep trouble.

"When did you know about the particular situation, and if you knew about it, why didn't you do something about it then? And, if you didn't know about it, why didn't you?"

The first and the second episodes at the beginning of this chapter illustrate another fundamental point with respect to all crises. In virtually every crisis situation, there is *always at least one other person* internal to, or inside, an organization who "knows for sure" about what is going on far in advance of the external public. There is always a "Linda Tripp" behind the scenes just waiting to gum up the works. It is not only parties *external* to an institution who will ultimately find out the truth, but they will find out precisely because there are *always* internal confidants or disgruntled employees who know what is going on.

In the end, the sixty-four trillion dollar question is, "We say we want honest leaders who can tell us the truth, but how much truth are we prepared to hear? How much can we bear?"

As is so often the case, our best poets have a deeper understanding of the human condition than our best social scientists. In one of his most shrewd observations about humankind the great poet T. S. Eliot observed: "Humankind cannot bear much reality."

Human truths come in an incredible variety of shapes and forms. There are ugly truths, beautiful truths, trivial as well as important ones, comforting truths, and disturbing truths as well. There are even, as modern physics has shown us, strange truths (black holes, chaos theory). The most important truths are those that are ethical and spiritual. These are the ones that give us the strength to face the unpleasant and to change.

For this reason, Ghandi could well contend that the "other person" who "knows" the truth about a person is not just that person's inner conscious, or superego as Freud put it; in a more profound sense, it is the "spiritual other" that is one of the deepest aspects of all human beings.[8] Indeed, it is precisely this "spiritual other" that makes all of us human. In this regard, there is always an "other" who needs to be taken into account.

It is also important to note that Machiavelli represents the ethics of "survival"; as such, it is a minimalist ethics. That is, one should always do the "bare minimum and nothing more." On the other hand, in terms of ethics our other three advisors are "maximizers" in the sense that they are concerned with the greatest development of the social, ethical, and spiritual sides of human beings and societies.[9] In addition, they also represent different points along the spectrum regarding whether or not to tell the truth, and how much of the truth to tell. Indeed, they are of special interest for precisely this reason. In effect, they stake out various points along the spectrum.

It is also vitally important to note that even Freud does not and in fact never would advise one to completely shed all of one's clothing in public. Freud recognizes explicitly that it is not necessarily in the best interests of a person to tell every dark and revealing secret about one's person. If anything, Freud calls for the cultivation of a very special relationship between two people, the therapist and the person who is the object of therapy. This is done so that acting together they can discover the truth about a person, and hence, discuss what indeed should be revealed to others.

To Freud we also owe the insight that people will invent the most elaborate fictions, and concoct the most incredible stories, to convince themselves of the "truth" of their fictions. In this sense, the biggest delusion of all is that one can indeed "know" things about one's self without any need of others. In other words, both "knowing" and the "truth" are only obtained through community, and at the very least, through the cultivation of a deep friendship with at least one other person. "Knowledge" and the "truth" are not the properties of a single mind in isolation and removed from others.

When, how much, and what kinds of truth does one tell?

After all is said and done, the point still stands that in today's world, there are precious few secrets anymore. Thus, the primary question still remains: "When, how much, and what kinds of truth does one tell?"

No matter what the crisis situation, I always advise my clients to tell as much of the truth about themselves as they are able and willing to tell. I next ask them to take the additional step and tell a bit more, and a bit more, etc. Only after both of us are satisfied that they have indeed told "enough" of the truth to ensure that the crisis will not be perpetuated any further can they finally stop. In short, how much "truth" do I tell my clients to reveal about themselves? More than they can stand to bear, but, unfortunately, not what the world wants to hear and to gloat over!

Finally, this chapter has deliberately employed the device of using four historical figures as theoretical crisis advisors, since they explicitly meet one of the most important needs of CM, i.e., the need for involving very different kinds of "voices." Indeed, they can be considered as very different from the usual stakeholders that are considered in most CM planning efforts. It is precisely the conversation and interplay between these different kinds of advisors that is the most needed, and unfortunately the element most often missing, from current CM efforts.

Strategy List for Chapter Four

- Examine the situation thoroughly.
- Avoid self-deception.
- Acknowledge responsibility for your product and actions.
- Realize that there are no secrets in the modern world.
- Use the Johari Window to analyze what you know about yourself and to help develop your potential.
- Realize that taking the initiative by telling the truth allows you to control who reveals the truth, in what circumstances, and when it is revealed.

Chapter Five

Assuming Responsibility

Victim or Villain?

"Last week, in a private meeting with Jewish supporters, Senator Al D'Amato called his opponent, Representative Charles Schumer, a 'putz head,' which is a vulgar Yiddish insult. When Schumer took umbrage, D'Amato offered this state-of-the-art response:

"STEP 1: Feign ignorance. 'I don't know. I

don't remember. It certainly was not for any public, ehh . . .'

"STEP 2: Deny it happened. 'I have no knowledge of ever doing it. I just don't. I think it's ridiculous . . . I would never, I have not engaged in that. I wouldn't engage in it. I haven't done it. Why am I going to do it now?'

"STEP 3: O.K., O.K., admit it. Although just in a private letter. Which somehow gets in the hands of the media: 'The Yiddish word I used to describe you at a private meeting means 'full.' '

"STEP 4: And even though you've completely ignored the common meaning of the word, pat yourself on the back for your courage. 'I stand by my remark 100%.'

"STEP 5: Now quickly blame the victim for being insulted. 'You are trying to twist that into a religious slur . . . I urge you to stop this transparent politically motivated attack.'

"STEP 6: Pray that with just a little more than a week to go until Election Day, the blunder isn't fatal."

"Campaign Textbook: How to Handle a Gaffe"
Time[1]

Chapter Four argued that effective CM is not a matter of following some mechanical formula or procedure. No framework for CM, no matter how comprehensive or good it is, can substitute for character and creativity. In slightly different words, effective CM is the *product* or the *multiple interaction* with a comprehensive framework *and* an organization's character *and* its creativity.

This chapter thus continues the exploration of additional stakeholders, and their attributes, that are critical to consider for effective CM.

Victim versus Villain

In almost all human-caused crises, there are only two major outcomes. You will either be perceived as a victim or cast as a villain. Once you are labeled a villain, it is extremely difficult, although not impossible, to shake the label. And even in the fortunate case where you are cast as a victim, it is still relatively easy to turn into a villain.

> *In almost all human-caused crises, there are only two major outcomes. You will either be perceived as a victim or cast as a villain.*

All things "being equal" (which is virtually never the case), most persons and organizations in crisis will tend over time to fall into the role of villain. It requires very little effort to be perceived as a villain or the bad guy. Conversely, it requires a great deal of effort to be perceived as a victim or the good guy. And it requires continually ongoing efforts to continue to be perceived as a victim.

Why do some people and organizations get tagged or naturally fall into the role of a victim, and why do others invariably get tagged as villains? Furthermore, once tagged as villains, how do some people and organizations manage to shake the labels? And, how do some people and organizations that are tagged as victims manage to maintain the roles? Clearly, the answer to the preceding questions cannot be, "Never do anything wrong!" for it is not in the nature of humans never to commit errors.

The Differences between Victims and Villains

The essential definition of a victim is a person, or organization, to whom harm is done, whether intentionally or not. A victim can also be a person who, unintentionally or unknowingly, causes harm to another. Further, a victim can also potentially be someone who causes harm to another person even though the victim did everything humanly possible to prevent it.

Common parlance differentiates between "liars" and "damn liars." By the same token, there are "villains" and "damn villains." A villain is someone who knowingly causes, or allows, harm to another. Damn villains are those who knowingly cause harm to another and then deny that they did it or act to evade assuming responsibility for their actions or inactions.

"Recovered" or "repentant" villains acknowledge forthrightly what they did, accept full responsibility for their actions, promise to correct the situation, promise never to repeat it, and finally, ensure actions to enforce their promises. "Damningly damnable villains" engage repeatedly in stonewalling or denial, such that they compound the original crisis, thereby setting off a chain reaction of additional crises in response to the initial one.

Guaranteed Ways to Become a "Damningly Damnable Villain"

There is no doubt that one of the most horrendous things about villains is not merely that they are full of denial, but that their denial takes the particularly odious form of their acting like they were the real victims of a crisis. They not only fail to own up to their own behavior, but they act as though the real crisis is what has happened to them.

So rare is the act of owning up that when it happens from time to time we are truly shocked. In responding to the (substantiated) charges that Chrysler falsely reset odometers on its cars, Lee Iacocca's response was a model of brevity. He said: "It happened; it shouldn't have happened; it won't happen again." Notice carefully that Iacocca broke the inevitable and vicious pattern that often results when one denies responsibility. He broke it by forthrightly assuming responsibility for what happened. He thus prevented the initial crisis from turning into a chain reaction of further crises. If one does not assume responsibility right from the very beginning, then a chain reaction is virtually guaranteed. It is not necessarily the initial crisis that gets one into trouble, but it is the chain reactions of further crises that result from the deepening of a mess.

Dumb Arguments: USAir

Those who are thrust into the role of a villain invariably use convoluted, dubious, "dumb" arguments, or "clever half-truths," to deflect criticism and to deny their responsibility. For instance, when USAir experienced five crashes in five years, USAir's CEO, Seth Schofield, said that each crash was completely independent of the others. In other words, there was no pattern of statistical association among the five crashes. To underscore his belief in the safety of USAir, Schofield said that he would have no hesitation whatsoever in having his family fly on the airline. Whereas his statement was obviously meant to assuage the fears of the public, it could well have produced the exact opposite result. Offering to fly his family was obviously meant as a gesture to reassure the public, but it very well could have communicated just the opposite, i.e., that he was foolhardy and willing to risk the lives of his loved ones!

The basic premise that underlies Schofield's argument is truly incredible, since it assumes that everyone is a "rational statistician." One should confront the statistic of five crashes in five years by accepting the "fact" or the "premise" that each of them is statistically independent of one another; that is, none of the crashes have anything whatsoever to do with one another. Such arguments not only fail to react to the deep-felt anxieties of humans, but they actually perpetuate them.

One of the most basic lessons of CM is that one should never—repeat never!—give technical explanations or impersonal statistics to assuage the fears of consumers. Technical information is more likely than not to be perceived as gobbledygook, a sure sign that one is engaged in hiding the truth, and indeed has truth to hide. Thus it serves only to further the crisis.

One should never—repeat never!—give technical explanations or impersonal statistics to assuage the fears of consumers.

One of the most interesting aspects of the USAir crashes was an investigative analysis by a *New York Times* reporter. First of all, his report shows that once again there are no secrets in today's world. As any good investigator would do, he dug in and interviewed a number of people in the USAir system. What he found was so revealing and shocking that it made the front page of the newspaper.[2]

Like so many of today's organizations, USAir was the result of mergers among several airlines. One of the worst outcomes of a merger is unfortunately something that is rarely scrutinized. It is well known that different organizations tend to have very different "safety cultures." Merging such cultures is not easy, for they often think quite differently about safety and have quite different safety standards. For instance, while in theory all organizations are supposed to meet the minimum standards set by the FAA, organizations differ considerably in the amount that they exceed the minimum standard.

An important factor in the creation of USAir through mergers is that it occurred in the first place because of the desire to cut costs. One of the most frightening aspects of many corporate mergers is that safety is often one of the very first things that is seriously cut or compromised. While this does not and need not happen in every case, it happens enough that the public has good reason to be worried.

The *New York Times* article argued that whether the crashes were independent of one another was really beside the point. For instance, one thing was certainly common to all of the crashes: USAir's management system. It surfaced that on numerous occasions, USAir flights were forced to request emergency landings because the airplanes were flying without enough fuel. This is very disturbing since one of the very first items on the preflight safety checklist is whether there is enough fuel aboard a plane. And in fact, on numerous occasions, USAir pilots lied about why they were requesting emergency landing.

The investigative reporter found that there was indeed a "common pattern" across all of the accidents. In effect, a "safety culture" had become a "crisis-prone culture."

Flawed Reasoning: Intel

Some of the same kinds of errors—i.e., flawed reasoning—were committed by Intel when it was faced with a flaw in its computer chips. Instead of replacing all chips without questions asked, Intel put the burden on its customers to prove to Intel's satisfaction that a customer's application was "critical enough" to warrant replacement. The unstated assumption by Intel's top management was that "everyone is an engineer" or

Intel's . . . failure was to respond to people as human beings who needed "emotional reassurance" that their trust could be placed in a particular product.

"thinks like an engineer." That is, in terms of the ways in which engineers think, no "rational person" would want a replacement if one was not "rationally warranted."

Once again, the failure was to respond to people as human beings who needed "emotional assurance" that their trust could be placed in a particular product. Of course, one can argue that running a computer application is not as dangerous as flying in a plane. However, it ignores the fact that computers are used in highly critical situations, such as by hospitals or air traffic controllers. In this sense, flaws in a computer application can indeed have dangerous consequences.

Another Lesson Learned from USAir and Intel

The cases of USAir and Intel illustrate another important lesson, one that was stressed in the last chapter: One almost invariably ends up doing later—as a crisis unfolds and becomes much worse—the very thing one stated one would never do in the beginning of the crisis. For instance, in the case of USAir, it later hired an outside crisis and safety consultant to inspect the safety requirements of the total USAir system. In Intel's case, it later made an unconditional offer to replace all chips, no questions asked. However, by then, the number of chips that it had to replace potentially was much greater than if it had made the offer initially without any constraints. Thus, while I cannot prove that in all cases one will be forced to do what one has refused to do in the beginning, there is a clear trend. The burden, in other words, is on the person and the organization to prove that it will not be forced to do later what it has refused to do in the very beginning.

While telling the truth may be damaging and hurtful to one's character and reputation, it is often one of the very few strategies open to someone in the heat of a major crisis. While it cannot be guaranteed that such a strategy will always win in the court of public opinion, it is often the only viable option.

One thing above all is clear. Continued denial will ensure that one will lose in the court of public opinion, and hence, become and remain a villain. One always needs to bear in mind that there are multiple courts in which one is being tried. First, there is the court of law. Second, there is the court of public opinion. Third, there is the stock market and other societal institutions. While lawyers may prevail in helping one survive the legal system—and even this is not guaranteed—the pursuit of legal strategies alone is likely to doom one to fail in the wider court of public opinion.

Continued denial will ensure that one will lose in the court of public opinion, and hence, become and remain a villain.

Vigorous Denial: ValuJet

The all-time worst example of villainy may well be that of Lewis Jordan, president of the ill-fated and by now defunct airline ValuJet. From the very beginning of the crash of a ValuJet airliner in the Florida Everglades, Jordan denied vigorously that *any* aspects of ValuJet's operations were defective. As a result, Jordan literally set himself up by waving the proverbial "red flag" for everyone to investigate thoroughly whether his contentions were true. Instead of admitting problems from the very beginning, he repeatedly claimed that his airline was free from defects.

The case of ValuJet is worth examining in detail. As ValuJet's crisis unfolded over months, I scrutinized every aspect of the extensive TV and print coverage to which I could gain access.

One of the most illuminating, and damaging, aspects of the case is contained in one of Jordan's very first interviews immediately after the crash on the Larry King show. At one point, King asked Jordan how he and his airline were responding to all the intense scrutiny by the media of ValuJet. In responding to King, Jordan committed a classic Freudian slip. He said: "Well, after all, it [intense media scrutiny] comes with the territory. We're in a business where we *take* [italics mine] the lives of people." He obviously meant to say, "We safeguard the lives of people given to us in trust."

A few minutes later, Jordan committed another Freudian slip. In response to a question by King asking him how competitive ValuJet's wages were and how profitable ValuJet was in the industry, Jordan said: "We pay the lowest wages." Once again, it is clear from the general context that he obviously meant to say we have the "lowest prices" of any airline in the industry.

These slips, of course, stand in marked contrast to Jordan's earlier claims with regard to the safety of ValuJet. When it was later confirmed that ValuJet farmed its maintenance out to the lowest bidders, Jordan lost what little remaining credibility he still possessed.

One of the saddest and most tawdry aspects of the ValuJet crisis occurred a few months after the crash. CNN filmed a meeting between ValuJet's top officers and its employees. In one scene, ValuJet's chief corporate counsel reacted angrily to the media because it had portrayed ValuJet as the villain. He is seen proclaiming in front of his employees that they were "the true victims of the situation."

Proclaiming that ValuJet was the victim was not only disingenuous, but morally outrageous. How could the airline claim to be the victim instead of the 110 persons who died in the Florida Everglades under the worst of conditions?

What happened on the Larry King Show was not an isolated incident. On more than one occasion, Ted Koppel of ABC's Nightline pressed Jordan repeatedly as to whether there were any aspects of ValuJet's operations that were not up to par, and might even be at fault. In every case, Jordan denied any culpability. From a legal standpoint, one can understand Jordan's denial. Nonetheless, even if he won in the court of legal opinion, he more than lost in the court of public opinion. Indeed, the airline finally lost in the biggest court of public opinion, the stock market, when it was forced to declare bankruptcy.

Ignoring the Human Side: Intel

Because the case of Intel is important, it is also important to review it in a bit more detail. Intel, the manufacturer of Pentium chips, was forced, after first staunchly refusing, to recall all of its chips when they were discovered to contain a flaw that affected complex division problems.

The flaw was first discovered by an obscure mathematician. He was performing esoteric calculations with prime numbers (numbers that are divisible only by 1 or themselves, for example, 1, 3, 5, 7, and so on). The area of mathematics in which he was working necessitated performing billions of computations on ten-digit numbers. Intel claimed that the errors associated with its chips were extremely rare. They would show up only in every few billion calculations. But since the professor was performing billions of calculations, he was in a perfect position to discover the problem. The error later turned out to be more common than Intel first admitted.

The professor alerted Intel, and after receiving an unsatisfactory response, he went public. He used the Internet to alert others and to inquire whether they experienced the flaw as well. The Internet was soon abuzz as others quickly discovered the error as well.

Intel refused to recall its chips even though customers were complaining strongly. In effect, Intel put the burden on its customers to prove that their applications were critical enough to warrant a replacement chip. What a clever marketing and public relations (PR) ploy! What better way to quickly alienate one's customers.

The situation quickly escalated in to a crisis when IBM, which used Pentium chips in its personal computers, announced that it would no longer utilize Intel's chips. Only after the howls of protest from consumers reached a crescendo did the company finally agree to replace all chips, no questions asked. By then, Intel had created a PR nightmare for itself.

This case is a model for how *not* to manage a crisis. First, it is never advisable to alienate one's customers. As obvious as this seems to be, it was not obvious to the engineering culture that drives Intel. To Intel's engineers, the customers were "reacting emotionally," and hence, "irrationally." Intel's engineers reasoned as follows: "If a customer's application wasn't critical enough to warrant a replacement, why then would he or she *rationally* want one?" By eschewing emotions, Intel's engineers were unable to understand the reactions of its customers.

The Intel case is a model for how not *to manage a crisis.*

Intel defined its problems in purely technical terms, as a computer applications problem. It did not define it in human terms: Users had fears and anxieties that needed explicit acknowledgment and attention. Without this attention, one of the most vital links in the chain between the manufacturer and its customers—trust—was broken. As a result, Intel committed one of the most basic errors associated with problem solving: *solving the wrong problem precisely*![3] It defined its problem primarily as a technical one when it was in fact both a technical *and* a human one.

Saddest of all, this story shows that Intel, one of the companies most responsible for thrusting us into the Systems Age, doesn't really understand systems. In this sense, it certainly does not understand the "systems factor" that is one of the components of the CM framework that we introduced in Chapter Three.

I cannot emphasize enough that no matter how complex they are, systems are not composed of technologies alone. Instead, systems *are* the *interactions* among organizations, people, and technologies. While technologies may be rational—and even this is assuming a great deal—organizations and people are certainly not completely rational.

No matter how complex they are, systems are not composed of technologies alone. Instead, systems are *the* interactions *among organizations, people, and technologies.*

In sum, Intel defined its initial problem using too narrow a set of disciplines—in this case primarily only engineering and technology. The inevitable consequence was that the problem quickly turned to a major crisis, which ended up costing the company half a billion dollars, much more than it would have if Intel had initially offered to replace all its chips with no questions asked.

Should One Always Admit Responsibility?

The moral of this and the preceding chapter is *not* that every individual and organization should admit responsibility and disclose the worst about itself whenever it is challenged. It does mean that if one chooses *not* to admit or *not* to tell the complete truth with regard to a specific charge, then one better have a very, very strong case to justify and to support one's position. If one indeed has "all the facts" to back up that what one did was the correct thing to do, or, if one can clearly prove that one is not guilty of the charges at hand, then obviously no one is asking that an individual or an organization roll over and play patsy. Such a recommendation is patently absurd! However, if there is *any* truth whatsoever to the charges, then I *unequivocally* advise the individual or organization to admit their culpability, put the crisis behind them, and get on with business.

In spite of this, no one can guarantee that coming "absolutely clean" will stop a crisis dead in its tracks. Nonetheless, I believe that the public is far more forgiving of someone who forthrightly admits his or her guilt and promises sincerely to correct it, and most of all, who follows through on those promises, than of one who continues to engage in evasion or denial. The case of Richard Nixon is testimony to what happens when one does not come clean, and indeed, engages in distortion and worsening denial.

Can the Media Cover Its Own Crises?

To show how complicated and muddied the waters are, consider the following case. One of the most ironic aspects of telling the truth involves the news media, the very institution that "sticks it" to others when they don't follow its advice.

A few years ago, NBC was accused of staging tests that overrepresented the danger of GM trucks exploding upon being hit from the side. In the early days of crisis management, PR firms counseled organizations not to be antagonistic in their dealings with the media. Crisis experts advised organizations to send their top executives through media training so they could respond to tough questions under fire and not lose their cool. We urged them to be straight and candid with the media. We counseled them that "no comment" was a strict no-no and tantamount to an admission of guilt. We advised them that if they didn't know the answer to a particular question, they should get back to the appropriate person or persons when they did, such as Johnson & Johnson did in the Tylenol tamperings. Above all, we cautioned them again and again, "Don't be defensive; don't get mad or angry; it will only hurt you even more."

I am not so sure any longer whether this advice holds in its entirety, even though I have stated strongly that one should err on the side of coming clean. Ever since the NBC fiasco, I've observed that more and more organizations and top executives are not only beginning to fight back, but if they feel that they have good reason to believe that they have not done anything that would qualify as a crisis, then their attitude is that "they are not going to take it anymore." In short, they are not only willing to fight back, but in the direct words of one top executive with whom I spoke, "Every time the media calls, I view it as a declaration of war." Such sentiments are an expression of more than the perhaps natural hostility that organizations that have committed an impropriety typically feel towards the media. Something else is at work.

In the past, most organizations basically feared the media. They believed, correctly or not, that the media could make or break any organization at will, whether it was right or wrong. Indeed, whether one was "right" didn't really matter. Little wonder that organizations were naturally suspicious of and even hostile towards the media.

However, NBC's admission that it staged explosions with regard to GM trucks makes it a very different ball game, especially when the "truth" had to be dragged out of NBC. Organizations have always felt to a certain extent that "the media will distort and lie in order to sell papers or TV programs." Now, however, they feel that they have "real proof."

In the end, the power of all institutions rests not only on fear but on moral authority as well. When both of these qualities are lost, then no institution can command attention or respect.

For years, the media have successfully obliterated the lines between sports, news, and entertainment.[4] That is, they have blurred the line between "reality" and "fiction." As a result, they cannot retreat to the position that the NBC fiasco was merely an isolated episode of embellishing or "stretching the truth."

The true significance of the NBC flap is that it is a clear early warning signal that the media, which revel in covering the crises of others, have a significant one of their own brewing. One cannot perpetually cross over the line between reality and re-creations of it and continue to believe that it will have no serious repercussions.[5] One cannot distort or manufacture reality at will. If the media want to continue to remain the "objective" watchdog of society, they must cover their own crises with the same vigor that they cover those of others.

In short, isn't it time for the news media to learn the very same lessons that they have forced on others: In today's world, there are no secrets?

Strategy List for Chapter Five

- Assume responsibility for your actions or inactions.
- Do not act like the "real victim" of the crisis.
- Do not try to hide behind half-truths or dubious arguments.
- Never give technical explanations to assuage the fears of customers.
- Respond to the emotional reactions of the victims.
- Don't assume that the public will use the same logic as your organization.
- Avoid alienating the victims, customers, or stockholders.
- Recognize that telling the truth may not stop a crisis from developing.

Chapter Six

Detecting Weak Signals

Making Sure That You Are the First to Get the Worst News!

"Failure does not strike like a bolt from the blue; it develops gradually according to its own logic. (C)omplicated situations seem to elicit habits of thought that set failure in motion from the beginning. From that point, the continuing complexity of the task and the growing apprehension of failure encourage methods of decision making that make failure even more likely and then inevitable.

We can learn, however. People court failure in predictable ways . . ."

Dietrich Dörner, *The Logic of Failure*[1]

In the last chapter, I argued that assuming responsibility is not solely or merely a matter of telling the truth, acknowledging the consequences of one's actions or inactions, or saying that one is sorry. As important as these are, effective crisis management is much more a matter of putting the appropriate mechanisms in place *prior to* a crisis that will help reduce the chances of a crisis and managing it more effectively once one has occurred.

Once again, it is instructive to consider Machiavelli as a prominent crises advisor. I can well imagine his stating the thesis of this chapter as follows:

> **Machiavelli:** *Dear Prince, you are extremely well advised to listen closely to all of the signals, however faint, of impending bad news. They are your only first line of defense. You need to constantly scan your kingdom for signals of bad things that are about to happen, whether they are of your doing or someone else's. This is the only chance you have to gain advantage.*

> *Therefore, set up throughout your kingdom ears and eyes that can pick up the weakest signals before they are apparent to your enemies. Furthermore, you must have couriers transmit on a steady basis the results of these ears and eyes to a central location in your palace so that you can see what patterns, if any, are emerging from the haze. I advise you to err on the side of acting on bad news, i.e., admitting that you may have been responsible for a bad situation instead of stonewalling it. Therefore, my lesson is to pick up bad news before others do, admit your responsibility as soon as possible, and undertake those actions to correct the situation.*

The Importance of Signals

Prior to their actual occurrence, all crises send out a repeated train of early warning signals. If these signals can be picked up, amplified, and acted upon, then many crises can be averted before they happen. True, in many cases, the signals are weak and filled with noise. Nonetheless, it usually turns out that there is at least one person in every organization who knows about an impending crisis. The problem is that those who often know most about it are the ones who have the least power to bring it to the attention of the organization.

The Space Shuttle Challenger

One of the most important examples of signal detection pertains to the tragic explosion of the space shuttle Challenger with the resulting loss of seven lives. The Presidential Commission Report into the causes of the accident found in no uncertain terms that the technical cause was the faulty O-ring design. However, even more serious was a faulty organization that prevented those who had serious doubts about the adequacy of the design from being heard. In effect, their voices and concerns were prevented from getting to the top of the organization. The case of the space shuttle thus shows that it is one thing to have "weak signals." It is quite another to have them blocked by an organization. It is for good reason that organizations that deliberately block signals deserve the label "crisis prone."

The case of the space shuttle Challenger is a tragic example. The Appendix to the Presidential Commission Report contains an "audit" of a string of memos that failed to make it from the bowels of the organization to the top. One of the most revealing memos begins with the painful cry "Help!" In no uncertain terms, the memo says that if the space shuttle continues to fly with the current design, then a disaster is virtually guaranteed to happen. The Presidential Commission Report shows all too well how an organization that exercises power and creativity in blocking bad news, rather than in attending to it, is guaranteed to produce a disaster. This is one of the saddest cases I know of, where an organization had clear signals of bad news and then deliberately chose to block them.

Ignoring the Warnings

Consider another case: My colleagues and I had occasion to audit a power utility that served extreme northern settlements. It was literally the case that if the electric power failed to these communities, they only had twenty-four to thirty-six hours before their inhabitants would freeze to death. In performing a crisis audit of the utility, it turned out that those most likely to find potential flaws in the electrical generators that served the communities were maintenance workers. At the end of each shift, these workers filled out a log. In theory, the logs were then read by the workers' supervisors. However, in practice, the logs were almost never scrutinized. In exploring this situation, we found that maintenance operators had the lowest status of any person in the organization. As a result, their warnings were not taken seriously.

The Challenger disaster is one of the saddest cases I know of, where an organization had clear signals of bad news and then deliberately chose to block them.

What is so sad and tragic about this particular situation is that it illustrates precisely the essential differences between natural and human-caused disasters. The status of maintenance operators is conferred by humans. It is not dictated by Mother Nature. The roles, functions, and jobs in organizations are the result of human decisions, not God's.

This story also illustrates another important point. People are not stupid. They do exactly what they are rewarded for, and as a result, they know exactly what is rewarded. Organizations thus get exactly the behavior they reward. If something is relatively unimportant or regarded as such, then people don't take it very seriously.

The case of the utility has another unsavory aspect that adds to the potential tragedy. Linemen had the highest prestige of anyone in the organization. In climbing poles to repair lines, they almost always chose *not* to wear safety equipment. In fact, the job of a lineman typically attracted people who couldn't wait to take risks. Part of the "thrill" of the job was to see how much one could get away with by not wearing necessary safety equipment. In effect, being "crisis prone" was an unstated job requirement. Little wonder that maintenance operators were not perceived in the same light. They were not macho enough!

A typical objection that my colleagues and I have encountered repeatedly is a rationalization, which, like all particular rationalizations, contains a grain of truth. This rationalization, another example of cultural denial we discussed in Chapter Three, is the contention that all organizations contain so many signals that it would be impossible to attend to every one of them. Thus, if one attended to such signals, one would need to attend to them all of the time, and this would inevitably crowd out the necessary work that needs to get done.

Whatever truth this rationalization contains, it obscures a basic point. Whenever it is in our direct interest, we humans can search out and magnify the most insignificant of signals.

For instance, consider the following. Most humans are naturally intensely interested in finding life on other planets. The verification that such life exists, especially higher-order, intelligent life, as well as successful contact with it, would be one of the most eventful moments in human history. As a result, huge electronic telescopes have been set up in conjunction with complex computers to constantly monitor signals from outer space. The computers work by noticing the most minute signals that deviate from "normal background noise," which is always present in the sky. To do this necessitates monitoring, as well as noticing, minute "blips" in literally millions of signals. The point is that humans can pick up the most minute signals when it is in their interest, whether to satisfy curiosity, imagination, or security needs.

The Case of a Major Insurance Company

Dr. Judy Clair, who teaches at Boston College, did her Ph.D. dissertation (under my supervision) on "signal detection in a large insurance company.'' The particular insurance company did a significant amount of work involving government Medicaid payments. Literally billions of dollars flowed through its operations annually. Given the presence of such large amounts of money, the temptation to commit fraud was always extremely high. Indeed, the top executives of the company made the reasonable assumption that if they had not recently encountered a fraud scheme, then it was not because it wasn't happening. It was only because they hadn't picked up on the latest scam. As a result, picking up signals of potential fraud schemes ranked high in the organization.

As a result of her research, Dr. Clair found a number of important things with regard to signals in organizations. While many of them are perhaps obvious, they are all important nonetheless. Indeed, their obviousness may prevent us from realizing their true importance.

The first point about signal detection is that to detect a signal, one needs to have detectors. As obvious as this may be, it is apparently not obvious enough, since most organizations do not have signal detectors.

The best way to think about detectors is in terms of a radio. If a radio is tuned to one and only one frequency, then it obviously only picks up signals that are broadcast on exactly that frequency. It does not pick up programs broadcast on other frequencies.

The point is that different types of crises send out very different types of signals. For this reason, every organization has to ask itself the following: ''What would count as a signal of the impending or near occurrence of a particular type of crisis?'' For instance, a pattern of slow, but noticeable, increases in the accident rate at an oil refinery may be a potential signal of an impending serious accident, such as an oil spill, fire, or explosion. Or, increasing amounts of graffiti scribbled on the walls of toilets and an increase in the number of sick jokes that are passed around an organization may be signals of impending employee unrest and sabotage. Once again, the point is that different crises have different kinds of signals associated with them. We would not expect signals that are signs of product tampering to be the same as signals of the breakdown of critical equipment, although the two can be related.

Different types of crises send out very different types of signals. Every organization has to ask itself: "What would count as a signal of the impending or near occurrence of a particular type of crisis?

The Dimensions of Signals

Signals can be differentiated along two dimensions. The first dimension pertains to the source of a signal. The second pertains to the kind of signal.

With regard to the first dimension, signals of impending trouble can originate from either inside or outside an organization. With regard to the second dimension, signals can be either technical (they are recorded by remote sensing devices), or noticed by people. In general, all four kinds of signals apply to every organization. Thus:

1. Internal technical signals
2. Internal people signals
3. External technical signals
4. External people signals

Internal technical signals are those that are recorded by technical monitoring devices, such as monitoring hazardous operations, possibly in remote locations. External technical signals can be recorded by community monitoring signals, such as environmental activist groups, in the immediate area surrounding a manufacturing plant. Internal people signals often come from the people working inside of a plant, such as the maintenance operators in the utility discussed earlier. External people signals often come from people living in the immediate vicinity surrounding a plant, who, for example, may literally "smell" that something is wrong.

Dr. Clair naturally found that if an organization doesn't have any kind of signal detector, then the probability of picking up a signal is virtually nil.

The Intensity Threshhold

The second stage in the "signal detection chain" is that once a signal is picked up, it must cross an "intensity threshold" in order to be recognized as such. In other words, every signal detector must be "calibrated." It must be set up to observe what is clearly in the "danger" or "potential danger" region. This means that criteria must be specified such that if the criteria are exceeded, then an alarm must go off.

Signals go off all the time in organizations, but because there is no one there to recognize them, record them, or attend to them, then for all practical reasons the signals are "not heard."

Once an alarm is sounded, then it must be heard by the right person, organization, or instrument. As trivial as this sounds, it is anything but trivial, especially in complex organizations. Signals go off all the time in organizations, but because there is no one there to recognize them, record them, or attend to them, then for all practical reasons the signals are "not heard."

What Can Happen

A few years ago, on an extremely hot day, a brownout occurred in New York City due to an overload on the city's power system, ConEd. Because AT&T is dependent upon ConEd to provide the power to run its electronic communication systems, AT&T experienced a breakdown.

Two of AT&T's systems that depend on ConEd are extremely critical because they provide the information for the air traffic control systems for La Guardia and Kennedy airports. When the brownout occurred, the power to AT&T's system dropped. A backup generator automatically kicked in. As is so often the case with complex systems, however, the generator failed. Fortunately, there was a backup to the backup in the form of a battery with a six-hour lifetime.

As soon as the battery kicked in, an alarm sounded to alert a human operator to monitor the life of the battery. Before six hours elapsed, the battery had to be replaced. Unfortunately, in this particular case no human operators were available to hear the alarm. By the time someone did hear it, six and one-half hours had elapsed. By then airplanes were circling dangerously in the air because the computer systems to bring them down safely were not functioning.

The irony of this whole situation is that the operators were not available to hear the alarm because they were attending a class on a new backup system!

Signal Transmission

Returning to Dr. Clair's research on signal detection, once a signal is heard, it has to be transmitted to the right people, as well as in the right form, so that people can take action. Unfortunately, if a signal does not relate to any of the daily, standard operating procedures of an organization, then even though it may be loud enough to be observed by many people, they may not know what to do about it. If it falls outside of the repertoire of known or expected behaviors, then people are at a loss what to do. For this reason, an important aspect of signal detection is the specification as to what potential problem a signal might relate, and further, if a signal is noted, what is to be done about it.

Next, according to Dr. Clair, even if a signal relates to a known problem in an organization, there must still be a clear reporting sequence. If one picks up a signal, but it is not known to whom one should send it, or, if the signal is sent but those to whom it is sent don't know what to do about it, then once again the signal will be ineffective.

Finally, it is not enough to pick up individual signals in isolation from one another. For instance, in many plants, one part of the operation may have a signal of a potential problem, and another may have another signal pertaining to another aspect of the problem. However, if these two signals are not sent to a central location point such that they can be pieced together into a larger whole, then the potential crisis may go undetected. In effect, one will not be able to see the "whole elephant" to which the separate signals pertain. In complex organizations, separate individual signals, no matter how loud, may not be sufficient to connote a problem. If in effect the signals "don't connect the dots," then we cannot and do not see a "problem."

As we mentioned in an earlier chapter, almost invariably there is at least one other person in every organization who "smells that something is rotten." Consider the cases of Barron's Bank and the bankruptcy of Orange County. In the case of Orange County, not only was the county's Treasurer, Robert L. Citron, implicated in the scandal, but also high-level officials from Merrill Lynch were implicated as well. Given the large numbers of persons who were involved in recommending and making risky investments for the county, it is inconceivable that no one at all knew in advance of the financial crisis that something was terribly wrong with Orange County's investments.

In complex organizations, separate individual signals, no matter how loud, may not be sufficient to connote a problem. If in effect the signals "don't connect the dots," then we cannot and do not see a "problem."

In the case of Barron's Bank, it is also inconceivable that a lone individual, a twenty-eight-year-old bank officer, could bring down a venerable institution with a 128-year history.

In both cases, Orange County and Barron's Bank, high-risk investments were being made with very little independent oversight. It strains the imagination to assume that no one knew what was occurring. In the case of Barron's Bank, it is almost as if the system was designed from the very beginning to hide signals. The young bank officer involved in making risky trades was both the executor of his activities as well as his own supervisor! Putting operational responsibility and oversight into a single job is thus almost a sure-fire prescription for disaster.

The case of Barron's Bank is also interesting for an additional reason. It shows how virtually all crises are linked to one another. In the case of Barron's Bank, the investments were made in Japan. They went sour when a major crisis, the Kobe earthquake, caused many of the investments to be called due. It thus showed not only how one type of disaster—a natural one—can affect another human-caused crisis, but that all disasters have human implications. At some point, all natural disasters involve human response systems. If those systems are poor, then they can contribute to a chain reaction of additional human-caused crises.

Strategy List for Chapter Six

- Do not deliberately block signals that would alert you to an impending crisis.
- Do not ignore warnings.
- Keep lines of communication open.
- Make sure you utilize signal detection mechanisms that are already in place.
- Reward signal detection and emphasize safety.
- Make sure your detection mechanisms search for signals from *all* seven types of crises listed in Chapter Three.
- Make sure your mechanisms are directed internally and externally, attuned to both technical and people signals.
- Make sure there is someone who is watching over these signals and who is ready to sound an alarm if necessary.
- Create a clear reporting sequence so that people know what to do in the event of a crisis.

Chapter Seven

Thinking Far Outside of the Boxes

"... the only cycle of life you can count on is the one that turns the unthinkable into the commonplace."

Randall Sullivan, "A Boy's Life, Part 2"
Rolling Stone[1]

Screw up once, and depending upon how understanding and forgiving the organization, it may be regarded as a "valuable learning experience," assuming of course that the company isn't destroyed in the process. Screw up twice, especially if it's the same "dumb error," and one is not likely to have the opportunity to do it again.

To err may be human, but to screw up repeatedly, or big time, is to preclude divine forgiveness.

All errors and mistakes are due fundamentally to making the wrong assumptions about business situations or people. "Smart mistakes" involve making assumptions that open up new, creative, and exciting possibilities. "Fatal mistakes or errors" involve assumptions that lead to disastrous outcomes.

This chapter shows how crisis management, which demands thinking about the unthinkable, is basically an exercise in creative thinking. It demonstrates the kind of thinking that is necessary via several striking examples. In particular, the chapter demonstrates the kinds of creative thinking and assumptions that are necessary if one is to prevent a major crisis from escalating.

Example 1: Benetton-Turkey

A few years ago, my wife and I had the opportunity to visit Istanbul, Turkey. This was well before the devastating earthquakes. While we were there, I was able to talk to several CEOs regarding recent crises they and their organizations had experienced. The most interesting was that of Benetton-Turkey.

For over fifteen years, the Turkish majority and the Kurdish minority have literally been at war with one another. The Kurds want to set up their own separate, ethnic state. As is so often the case, both sides have resorted to violence. Under the leadership of the Kurdish rebel Abdullah Ocalan (or Apo, as he is known) 30,000 Turks have been killed. In retaliation, untold numbers of Kurds have been killed or imprisoned and tortured.

For years, Apo has lived as a hunted man with a price on his head. In 1999 as the Turks were finally closing in on him, Apo fled to Moscow. Since Moscow wasn't anxious to receive him, given the thaw in the Cold War, he then fled to Italy, where he was welcomed warmly by the Italian Communist Party and unofficially by the Italian government.

When the Turkish government demanded that Apo be extradited, the Italian government refused, citing the fact that Turkey believes in the death penalty to which Italy is vehemently opposed. When Turkey promised to rescind the death penalty, Italy still refused to release Apo.

The reaction in Turkey was immediate. The Turkish people took to the streets in thousands to demonstrate against Italy and the innumerable Italian businesses that had Turkish subsidiaries. Italian flags were burned and demonstrators not only threatened to boycott Italian products, but to attack

Italian stores and products, such as Benetton, Ferrari, and Perelli.

As soon as the protests against Italian businesses that were situated in Turkey arose, most of the businesses reacted predictably, i.e., defensively. They took out newspaper ads to the effect that the Turkish people should differentiate between the Italian parent companies and the Turks who operated them. In other words, the ads presented "logical, rational arguments" as to why the Turks who operated Italian businesses should be treated differently.

From the vantage point of the people in the streets, the ads were totally nonsensical. As is typical of the vast majority of corporate responses, the ads basically assumed that the general populace would think like corporate executives. As we noted in a previous chapter, this is a common mistake.

Similar to the crises that befell USAir and Intel, corporate executives are constantly conditioned to and rewarded for thinking in terms of the "boxes" on their organization charts. As a result, they naturally think that everyone else should, and will, think this way too. They thus make the unpardonable assumption that "everyone thinks like us." But, as obvious as this may seem to them, "everyone" is not a corporate executive working for an Italian-based company!

Corporate executives are constantly conditioned to and rewarded for thinking in terms of the "boxes" on their organization charts. As a result, they naturally think that everyone else should, and will, think this way too.

There was, however, one company that did not respond in a knee-jerk fashion. It not only thought the unthinkable, but it actually did it. That company was Benetton-Turkey.

Benetton-Turkey was faced with the direct destruction of its stores, property, and substantial harm to its employees and customers. Reacting "with concern and speed," Benetton-Turkey's top "corporate response team"—composed of its president, head of public affairs, and head of corporate finance—decided that they should react emotionally to the situation, not merely rationally. As a result, they took the unprecedented step of taking out ads that sided *emotionally* with the Turkish people. The ads proclaimed: "First and foremost, we are Turks too! Our first allegiance and loyalty is to Turkey! We feel the same way that you do towards the Italians!"

Benetton-Turkey's top executives went even further. The next step was one of sheer brilliance. It demonstrates exactly what most companies are unable to think or do in the heat of a major crisis. As a result, it illustrates precisely the differences between "smart thinking" (including potentially "smart mistakes") and dumb thinking. That is, what Benetton-Turkey did is a premier example of a *potential* "smart mistake," for there was no surefire guarantee that the risky option they were to undertake would actually work.

Benetton-Turkey went to the heart of its hard-won and highly identifiable corporate logo. Over the years, Benetton had developed some of the most creative, attention-getting ads of any corporation. Indeed, because of its forceful, no-holds-barred approach, many of its ads have been the subject of controversy.

At the heart of its corporate identity—its logo—is the notion of "The United Colors of Benetton." This is meant to stand for the unification and integration of all people everywhere. Therefore, Benetton-Turkey reasoned that if it was to demonstrate convincingly that it sided *emotionally* with the Turks against Italy, then it had to make a clear symbolic statement. *As a result, it took the totally unprecedented action of removing the colors from its logo, at least in Turkey*! It also proclaimed strongly in extremely prominent ads that until the situation with Italy was settled, black wreaths would be placed on the storefronts of all Benetton stores throughout Turkey! In addition, all of the mannequins in its store windows would be dressed in black indicating that the company was in a state of "mourning!"

The response was instantaneous and overwhelming. The public responded so positively and with so much emotion that Post-it notes and poems were taped to the storefront windows of Benetton, indicating the public's deep and widespread support for Benetton-Turkey. The notes and poems proclaimed that the public understood that Benetton-Turkey was as much a victim as everyone else. It was certainly not the villain.

Naturally, before they undertook the risky step of putting wreaths on all of the storefronts, Benetton-Turkey's executives checked carefully with all of their store managers. All of the managers enthusiastically endorsed the plan of temporarily taking the colors out of Benetton.

To indicate their continued support of their store managers, Benetton-Turkey's executives also decided that they would not enforce normal financial requirements during the crisis. Its store revenues had plummeted dramatically as a result of the boycotts, but the stores were relieved indefinitely from meeting their financial quotas! This had the additional effect of building trust and camaraderie between Benetton's store managers and its top executives.

Because Benetton's actions were so completely out of the ordinary—so "outside of the boxes of traditional thinking"—I cannot overemphasize the creativity, as well as the riskiness, of both their thinking and their actions. Benetton went right to the heart of their corporate identity, their very reason for being, i.e., their colors. They decided that the most dramatic and visible act that they could take to demonstrate their emotional solidarity with the Turkish people was to remove, if only temporarily, their "colors."

Notice carefully what they did. They made the fundamental assumption that an act of defensiveness or of caution would not save the day. In effect, the executives of Benetton-Turkey assumed that they had to dramatically reverse a fundamental, taken-for-granted aspect of their corporate being. They thus flipped on its head one of the most fundamental underpinnings of their corporate existence. Needless to say, they did something that most businesses are almost totally unprepared to do. This is *not* to say that what they did was without considerable risk. But this is precisely what makes a person, a company, an institution, and even a country's acts potentially "heroic."

It is interesting to compare Benetton's actions with those of other Italian-based companies in Turkey, whose executives assumed implicitly that they were the "true victims" of the situation. As a result, they failed to acknowledge that the real victims were both the Turkish majority and the Kurdish minority. This is one of the most prevalent ways that companies commit mistakes that more often than not are fatal. Instead of identifying with the "true victims," they attempt to portray themselves as the "victims." The result is that they end up becoming the "true villains" of the entire affair.

The Moral of the Benetton-Turkey Story

◆ *Lesson #1*: Always respond first and primarily to the *emotional* needs of others (customers, clients, suppliers, employees). Later, and only later, respond rationally by giving reasons for your actions or supporting evidence, such as numbers.

◆ *Lesson #2*: Respond to the emotional needs of others as *they* perceive them, *not* as *you* perceive them.

◆ *Lesson #3:* One is not prepared to handle a major crisis unless one is able to do the unthinkable. In other words, coping with the unthinkable demands doing the unthinkable! To do this necessitates going to the core of one's corporate identity and flipping it on its head in order to make a highly dramatic and visible statement.

◆ *Lesson #4:* The fact that an organization like Benetton, or Johnson and Johnson, does well on one crisis in one part of the world is no guarantee that it will do well on other crises in other locations. In fact, this is precisely why an organization needs to have a central point where the lesson of crises worldwide can be stored and disseminated widely.

Example 2: The Make-a-Wish Foundation

For sixteen years, the Make-A-Wish Foundation has granted the wishes of terminally ill children. In the process, it has become one of the most respected charities worldwide. Recently, however, it was criticized severely for:

> [helping to arrange] what a teenager suffering from a brain tumor wanted most: to shoot a Kodiac bear in Alaska.
>
> But, [the Make-A-Wish Foundation] didn't blink. It turned to Safari Club International, which collected donations, including $4,000 in airline tickets,

> a Weatherby .340-magnum rifle, binoculars, hunting clothing, an outfitter, and a taxidermist.
>
> Now, the program that has provided thousands of families with joyful memories to help ease the depression of losing a child is on the hit list of virtually every animal-rights group in the nation.[2]

The decision to grant the teenager's wish is a tragic, but classic, example of the failure to think critically. The result is almost always the same: solving the wrong problem, and as a result, the creation of a major potential crisis for an organization.

> *The Make-a-Wish Foundation solved the wrong problem precisely and in the most effective way possible.*

If we assume that Safari Club International is the most effective way of achieving the teenager's wish, then the combined decision to grant the wish *and* to use Safari Club International is a premier example of *solving the wrong problem precisely and in the most efficient way possible*. It is also a prime example of muddled thinking, another of the reasons why things go wrong in organizations. It occurs because the assumptions that underlay the formulation of an important problem were not examined critically.

Since I don't actually know which assumptions were made by the foundation in attempting to justify its actions, I am thus not contending that my reconstruction of the arguments are those that were actually used. However, I do know from my work in CM that when an individual's or an organization's actions are onerous, or perceived as such, then it is up to the offending party to defend itself against the kinds of arguments that will most likely be used against it. In other words, the arguments I have constructed are not fanciful. They are based on my work in CM, which has taught me the kinds of attacks generated in response to an organization doing, or perceived to be doing, wrong.[3]

I believe that the foundation's most likely implicit, taken-for-granted assumptions were that the teenager was the primary stakeholder, and further, because of the tragedy of a life cut short, the outside world would be extremely tolerant of his last wish. To fully justify the foundation's decision, it would also have to assume that:

1. The wishes of a terminally ill child, no matter how dubious or onerous, warrant granting.

2. Other stakeholders will not object because of their sympathy for a dying child, or their sympathy will outweigh their ethical and moral qualms.

3. Other stakeholders will essentially see the situation as the foundation does: "How to grant the wish of a dying child as effectively as possible no matter how offensive it may be to others."

The all-too-common failure in such situations is the inability of an organization to anticipate and to gauge the reaction of a multitude of other stakeholders. The primary error is not merely the failure to "walk in their shoes," but far more seriously, the failure to "get inside their heads." This is precisely why decision makers need to continually take the pulse of a broad range of stakeholders with regard to important situations. This does not mean having a "perfect reading" of other people's minds; it merely means using market research and whatever other methods are available to check out one's taken-for-granted assumptions about a broad range of stakeholders.[4]

The Moral of the Make-a-Wish Foundation Story

- *Lesson #1*: *Never, never* assume that the outside world (persons outside of your immediate work group or family) will see a situation exactly as you do.

- *Lesson #2*: List as many assumptions as possible about as many stakeholders as you can think of. Be aware that the stakeholders you overlook, and especially the unwarranted assumptions that you are making about them, can come back to haunt you later.

- *Lesson #3*: *Never, never* solve the wrong problems precisely! In other words, always ask yourself, "Are we solving the wrong problem?"

Example 3: Walter von Wartburg of CIBA

When I first met Walter von Wartburg, he was head of Issues Management for the Swiss chemical conglomerate CIBA. Because CIBA takes issues management seriously, Walter reported directly to CIBA's president and CEO. Essentially, he is a top level "mess strategist" for the entire organization.

Some years ago at a CM conference in New York City, I heard Walter give a talk on issues management, illustrating it with several examples from CIBA. One in particular caught my fancy because it illustrates his novel approach to problem solving. It is particularly relevant here, since it is an excellent example of reaching out to and including stakeholders whose publicly stated goals are different from those of an organization.

A few years before, CIBA had been picketed by the German Green Party. Two party members had ascended a 600-foot smokestack and were in the process of unfurling a huge banner stating that CIBA was harmful to the environment. As Walter related the story, his eyes twinkled with amusement and excitement. He laughed as he said that the typical corporate response to such incidents would be, ''Red Bandit to Blue Bandit; locate the enemy and shoot them out of the skies!'' Walter was not only well aware of the typical response, but he was equally aware how it usually backfired, for it played precisely into the hands of the ''enemy.'' Worse, it created enemies where there were none before. He was thus determined to do something quite different.

Walter sent a corporate emissary up the smokestack to ask if the two Greens would come down because CIBA was worried about their safety. They could leave their banner up if they would just agree to talk and to come down. However, if they didn't want to come down, could CIBA at least help to ensure that they were properly anchored to the smokestack so that they wouldn't hurt themselves? The two Greens eventually agreed to come down and to talk over tea.

If the Greens had not responded to Walter's request to come down and engage in conversation, or if they had engaged in criminal actions, then the option of using force was always available. But why use force immediately without trying other options?

CIBA meets frequently with environmental groups and interest groups of all kinds. Although it does not agree with or give in to every demand, it does take what is said seriously. If there are charges that CIBA is polluting in a certain area, then CIBA conducts tests to verify the charges. If the charges are true, as they sometimes are, then CIBA fixes the problem instead of denying or dodging it.

Notice how CIBA's actions stand in sharp contrast to those of other prominent organizations, such as General Motors (Corvair), A. H. Robins (Dalkon Shield), and Nestlé (infant formula), which have all faced major crises.[5] In these cases, the offending organizations knew that they had serious problems of their own making (defective products), and yet, they chose to deny their problems vigorously by blaming them on consumers and troublemakers. Thus, the major strategy was one of impugning stakeholders instead of fixing problems.

The offending organizations knew that they had serious problems of their own making (defective products), and yet they chose to deny their problems vigorously by blaming them on consumers and troublemarkers.

Also notice the assumptions that were buried in Walter's strategy in responding to the Greens who had ascended CIBA's smokestack. He assumed that he and the Greens had enough in common that they could at least talk with one another. Further, by wanting to talk, he was assuming that what they had to say was relevant. As a result, Walter did not end up creating worse problems by solving the wrong one initially. In short, Walter didn't take the Greens' bait. What good would it have done for Walter to figure out the best way of storming CIBA's smokestack if storming is the solution to the wrong problem, and hence, highly likely to cause a major crisis for CIBA?

The Moral of the CIBA Story

◆ *Lesson #1*: Before adopting *any* proposed solution to a problem—especially all the more that it seems logical, rational, and eminently desirable—*always, always* ask, "Is the proposed solution likely to create even worse problems?"

Closing Remarks

One of the saddest facts about the current system of education is that it has abandoned its most fundamental reason for being. The main purpose of schooling at all levels is not to teach facts, which are constantly outdated anyway, but to teach critical thinking skills. Critical thinking not only allows us to respond to problems after they have occurred, but even more important, it allows us to anticipate problems before they are upon us, and hence, before it is too late to do anything about them.

A few years ago, Mark McCormack wrote a best seller entitled, *What They Don't Teach You at the Harvard Business School*.[6] The author only partially got it right. He was right that education fails to teach the necessary interpersonal skills, or what in today's world has been appropriately called *Emotional Intelligence*.[7] Unfortunately, schools generally fail to teach *both* "critical thinking" *integrated with* "emotional intelligence." Both of these things are vital in today's world. Without them, every organization is guaranteed to have a major crisis. Worse, it will have a string of crises from which it will likely not recover. On the other hand, those organizations that attempt to foster the "right critical thinking skills" are likely to gain a decisive advantage over their competitors.

The fatal error is not the commission of errors, for all of us are prone to mistakes. Rather, the fatal error is not to learn from our previous mistakes.

In the end, the fatal error is not the commission of errors, for all of us are prone to mistakes. Indeed, the commission of errors is fundamental to the human condition. Rather, the fatal error is not to learn from our previous mistakes. *As a matter of fact, as the following quote illustrates, most people have to be taught to commit errors, and not to avoid them altogether*!

> Many IS [Information Systems] managers say they encourage failure, but then don't back that up. Not [Barry] Lynn [Chief, Information Officer of Wells Fargo Bank]. To reflect this notion that failure is good, Lynn has a program he calls "Falling Forward," so named to demonstrate that falling can propel an individual—and an organization—to new successes. Each month, an internal publication at the bank has a falling forward story that gives kudos to those who have failed with honor (robustly, as it were).
>
> But Lynn does differentiate between types of failures. He breaks them down into two categories: stupid, uncaring failures, in which the individual who failed should be punished; and calculated risks or honest mistakes, which were risk-worthy and valuable learning experiences.
>
> The latter is the type of failure Lynn tolerates, even promotes.
>
> . . . Although failure is natural, we often take unnatural steps to avoid it. IS managers must reprogram their employees to accept failure. This was demonstrated to [Fred] Magee [Vice President and Research Director at Gartner Group, Inc., in Stamford, Connecticut] when he spoke with a CIO who asked a team of employees to work with customers to learn how to best use various technologies. He didn't want success stories, he wanted war stories—things that worked and especially, things that didn't.
>
> What didn't work was the project itself. The CIO

wanted his team members to learn from their failures. But they were programmed to succeed and felt uncomfortable with failure. So they refused to fail. "The team was incapable—without extra training—of failing," Magee says. "You will likely need to train your people to feel comfortable with failure."[8]

Strategy List for Chapter Seven

- Reward your employees for thinking out of the box.
- Search for new solutions to problems.
- Make sure the entire organization is behind your decisions.
- Consider relaxing company requirements in order to support your employees.
- Consider doing the unthinkable.
- Avoid solving the wrong problem.
- Check out your taken-for-granted assumptions about the stakeholders.
- Integrate critical thinking with emotional intelligence.
- Learn from previous mistakes.

Chapter Eight

Treating the Big Picture

"I always try to write on the principle of the iceberg. There is seven-eighths of it under water for every part that shows. . . . If a writer omits something because he does not know it, then there is a hole in the story."

Ernest Hemingway (interview in *Paris Review*)

To understand more fully what is so different about today's world, and as a result, why our problems require systems thinking if we are to formulate them effectively, let alone truly solve them, let us examine a highly simplistic, fictitious world. It is a world that does *not* require us to think systemically. When we understand why this world does not and could not really exist, we will be in a better position to understand the nature of today's world and hence why crisis management requires the ability to think systemically.

A Fictional World

First of all, we need to note that the world we are about to enter has never really existed. For this reason alone, it is most unfortunate that it is *the picture* that many people have in their heads when it comes to assigning and to accepting moral responsibility for their actions.

Let us begin by imagining, as Albert Einstein did many years ago in the initial, formative stages of his General Theory of Relativity, the case of an isolated rocket ship traveling deep in outer space. (Actually, Einstein used the mental picture, or "thought experiment," of an elevator. However, the difference is not crucial.) Next, imagine that the rocket ship is accelerating uniformly, namely that the force produced by the rocket's engine is smooth and constant (or, what amounts to the same thing, that the elevator is being pulled upwards by a constant force). Under these circumstances, the velocity of the rocket ship will continue to increase until it reaches the upper limiting speed of light. (Actually, it will only approach the speed of light since it would require an infinite amount of energy to travel as fast as light.)

Imagine further that the rocket is far from the gravitational pull of nearby planets, stars, or galaxies. Then, under these circumstances, the astronauts in the rocket ship would feel as if they were being tugged downwards by the constant pull of gravity of a real planet. In other words, the constant upward acceleration of the rocket would feel the same to the astronauts as if they were being constantly *tugged downwards* by gravity. Furthermore, since they were in outer space, there would be nothing for them to differentiate between the "virtual gravity" produced by the upward force of the rocket ship, and the "real gravity" of an actual planet. This would especially be the case if the inhabitants of the rocket ship, or elevator, had no portals or windows that would let them see outside.

Cause and Effect

Let us use Einstein's "imagined world" or "simple thought experiment" to illustrate the profound differences between the complex world in which we live and the simple, fictitious world of our imaginary rocket ship. Suppose, for instance, that the rocket ship were large enough to be luxurious, i.e., that it had an elaborate recreational room. Suppose further that the recreational room contained a pool table. Then, in this simple world, and *only* in this simple world, are there direct causes and effects. For example, if one of the astronauts were to pick up a cue stick and use it to hit a cue ball, and furthermore, if the cue ball hit the eight ball and caused it to drop into one of the side pockets, then we could say that the direct actions of the astronaut were the direct cause of the eight ball's moving and falling into the side pocket, i.e., the resulting end-effect. In this simple world, and only in this simple world, can one locate and assign direct causes and effects.

The world of the rocket ship constitutes a perfectly closed system. To account for the motion of the pool balls, it is not necessary to take anything into account except only those things going on inside the rocket ship. As a result, the behavior of the pool balls can be traced to the direct actions of one of the astronauts.

Exhibit 8-1 illustrates the nature of causality or a "cause-effect" relationship. In order for one thing, a cue ball, to be

Exhibit 8-1: A Simple Example of Cause and Effect

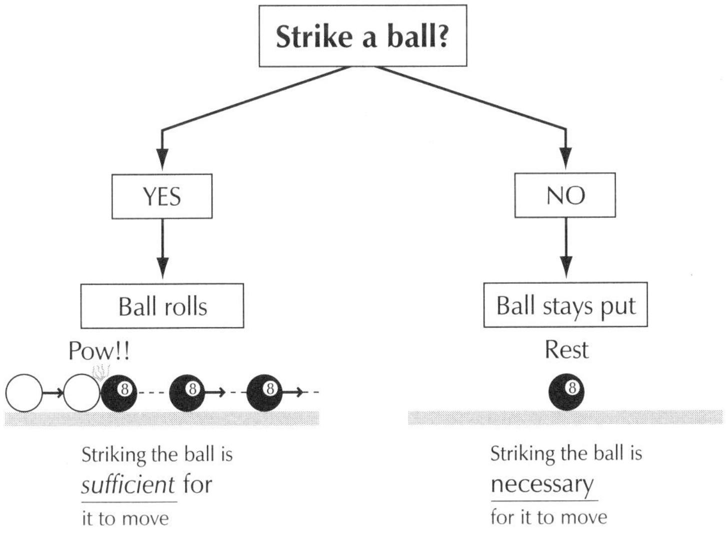

the cause of another thing, the motion of the eight ball, then the movement of the cue ball is both *necessary* and *sufficient* for the eight ball's subsequent motion. That is, in order for the eight ball to move, it is *absolutely necessary* that the cue ball, or some other object, *first strike it*. In somewhat different words, if the cue ball does *not* strike the eight ball, then the eight ball must *not* be capable of moving. On the other hand, if the cue ball strikes the eight ball, then this alone is *sufficient* for the eight ball to move. In other words, for the eight ball to move, nothing else is required than the cue ball. (Of course, the eight ball can move if something else strikes it.)

A cause-effect relationship is a very severe and limiting condition. Rarely is any one single thing sufficient to cause another thing. Furthermore, while a certain thing may be *necessary* for the occurrence of another thing, many other things are *required* as well. That is, rarely is one thing alone *sufficient* for the occurrence of another.

Rarely is any one single thing sufficient to cause another thing.

The whole point of the rocket ship example is that it does not apply in the complex world in which we live. In our world, there are no such things as single causes and effects. For instance, as we argued in the last chapter, we cannot say that one thing alone was the cause of the violence in Turkey. The conclusion is that every effect has multiple causes, and every set of causes produces multiple effects.

Edgar Singer and the Concept of Producer-Product

Edgar Singer is hardly a household name. Suffice it to say that in the words of his teacher, the great American philosopher

William James, "Singer is the best all-around student I have had in offering instruction in philosophy for some thirty years at Harvard." Singer went on to teach my philosophical mentor, C. West Churchman. I am thus fortunate enough to be able to trace my intellectual lineage directly back to one of the founders of pragmatism, the philosophical school in which I work.

In contradistinction to the limiting concept of cause-effect, which is much too simple to describe our world, Singer proposed instead the notion of "producer-product." A simple example of a producer-product relationship is one that in fact was used by Singer. It consists of the relationship between an acorn and an oak tree. An acorn is certainly *necessary* for the final production of an oak tree, but by itself, it is hardly *sufficient*. If we wish to get an oak tree, we certainly have to plant an acorn in the ground or in the soil. However, without the proper moisture, wind, and sun, an oak tree will not result. Thus, while an acorn may be "necessary" for the *production* of an oak tree, by itself it is *not* "sufficient." In slightly different words, we require many contributing factors if we are to produce an oak tree. The same is now true of all of the complex things that occur in society. Indeed, the necessity of many contributing factors is another of the major definitions of "complexity."

A Producer-Product Analysis of CM

It is sad to report that in all the years that I have worked in the field of CM, and in all the crisis audits that my colleagues and I have conducted for major corporations, there has only been one case of a corporate executive who was able to see the Big Picture, and as a result, able to understand how all the various contributing factors to various crises relate to one another. As a result, this particular executive was able to see the futility of preparing for individual crises in isolation, and furthermore, of attending to individual contributing factors in isolation as well. Since this point is so important, we need to take a brief look at the diagram produced by this executive. Of course, it should be understood that all explicit references to the executive and his organization have been disguised for reasons of confidentiality.

In all the years that I have worked in the field of CM there has only been one case of a corporate executive who was able to see the Big Picture, and as a result, able to understand how all the various contributing factors to various crises relate to one another.

Exhibit 8-2 shows what this executive considered to be major crises for the organization in which he worked. Although the distinction among the boxes is somewhat arbitrary, crises are shown as shaded boxes. On the other hand, effects, or contributing factors, are those things that lead up to and follow from crises, and these are shown as unshaded boxes.

This particular organization was in the oil industry. Hence, a major precipitating crisis for the organization was the falling of prices on world oil markets. This is shown as box 1 in the upper left-hand corner of the exhibit. The consequences of falling oil prices are shown as one proceeds through the rest of the exhibit. Hence, boxes 2, 3, and 4 show particular outcomes and additional crises that can result from falling oil prices. (Note that the numbers exist only for identification of the separate outcomes and crises, not for sequence.)

Exhibit 8-2: A Systems Map of Potential Crises

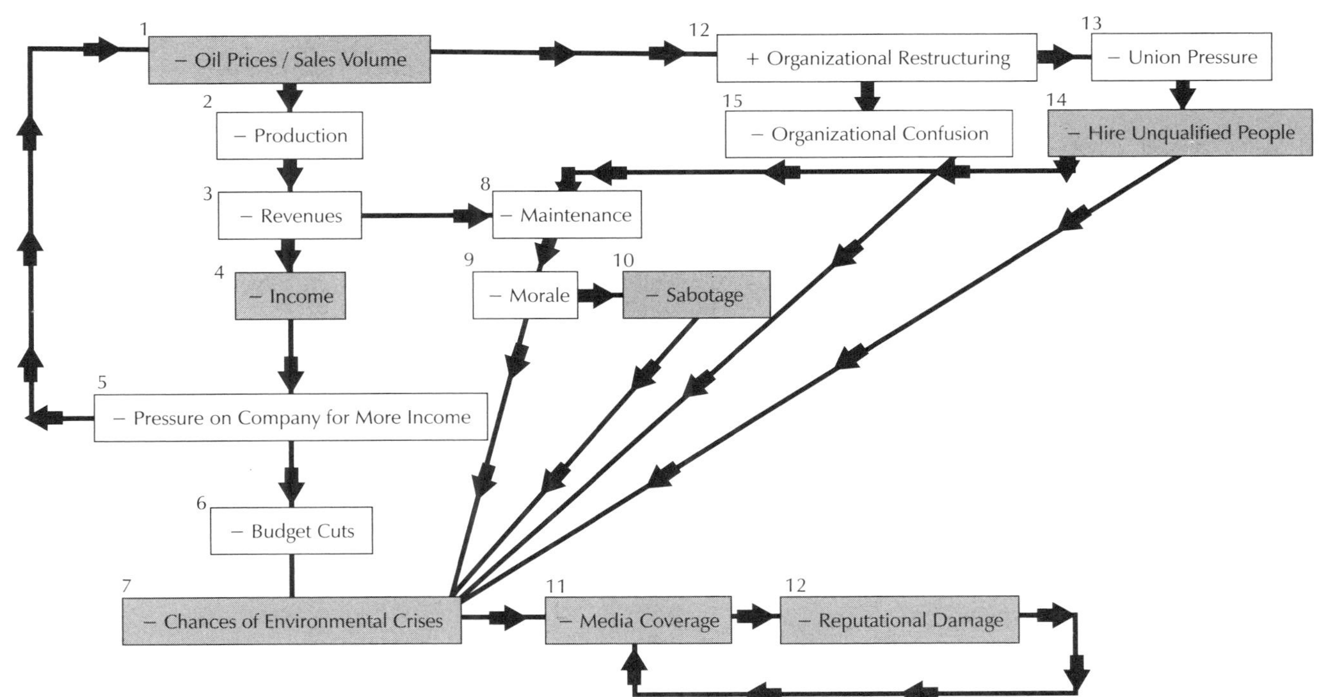

Exhibit 8-2 also shows what happens as other crises result from, and new, additional ones feed into, the drop in oil prices. As a result, the exhibit attempts to portray the complex set of relationships among various crises. The purpose is to give the organization a better overall map of the full array of forces it faces so that it can formulate actions and plans that will be most effective. Even more important, the purpose of the diagram is to help top level executives make sure that they do not take the wrong corrective actions, i.e., those actions that would actually make a crisis worse.

The Moral

Exhibit 8-3 represents a summary of the key themes we have discussed throughout this book. First of all, the rows are meant to indicate the differences between (1) those organizations that think and act systemically, and, (2) those that do not. It also is meant to portray the differences between (1)

Exhibit 8-3: A Decision Matrix

	Accept Responsibility	*Deny Responsibility*
Think and Act Systemically	1 Crisis prepared	2 A fundamental contradiction in terms
Do Not Think and Do Not Act Systemically	4 Luck? A lack of understanding may produce a chain reaction	3 Crisis prone, subject to a chain reaction of crises

those organizations that act responsibly, and (2) those that deny their responsibility.

Cell 1 is obviously the ideal case. Unfortunately, it still applies to only a small number of organizations. These are the very few that are prepared to think and to act systemically, and furthermore, accept their responsibility for crises. My colleagues and I call such organizations "crisis prepared" because they have done everything in their power to prepare for a wide variety of crises.[1] Not only does this mean that they have internalized the proper ways of thinking about crises, but it also means that they have put in place the appropriate crisis mechanisms such as early warning systems that will help them get a leg up on impending crises. Once again, this does not guarantee that they will never face a major crisis, for no such guarantee is possible. It does mean that when major crises occur, they will recover much faster than those organizations that are not prepared.

Cell 2 is a fundamental contradiction in terms. It is difficult to imagine that one can think and act systemically, and yet, deny one's responsibility. An important part of thinking and acting systemically is that it automatically includes the acceptance of responsibility. On the other hand, this does not mean that the situation shown in cell 2 can never occur, for a great deal hinges on what an organization believes thinking and acting systemically is.

Cell 3 represents those organizations that are of greatest concern. These are the organizations that neither think nor act systemically. They are the ones that are also most likely to deny their responsibilities. For this reason, my colleagues and I call such organizations "crisis prone."[2] They substantially increase the odds that they will experience a major crisis that will affect not only them, but also their customers and surrounding communities. The worst fear is that they will set off a chain reaction of additional crises that they will be unable to control.

And cell 4 typifies those organizations that constantly live on the edge. Whether they are aware of it or not, they count on luck to get them through any crisis. They neither think nor act systemically, and yet, somewhat paradoxically, they accept responsibility for their actions. The point is that in spite of their willingness to accept responsibility, their lack of thinking and acting systemically will nonetheless set off a chain reaction of crises that they will be unable to control. However, if by the acceptance of responsibility one means the implementation of the proper CM control mechanisms, then how is such a thing really possible without thinking systemically?

Finally, Exhibit 8-4 is an illustration of the things that all organizations can do to better prepare for major crises. The chart shows what one can do in the short-term versus the long-term. It also shows what one can do in order to be reactive as well as proactive with regard to major crises. In sum, Exhibit 8-4 is an ideal plan for the evolution and development of an effective program of CM for every organization.

Closing Remarks

In the end, we are faced with the fundamental question, "What is it that allows individuals and organizations to both accept responsibility and to prepare for crises?" The answer cannot be the precise determination of how much a particular factor contributes to a specific crisis. This is not to say that we should not try to gather the best possible data. But we must realize fundamentally that all data are at best incomplete. We live in a world that is far too complex to collect precise and perfect data on anything.

Exhibit 8-4: The Development of an Integrated CM Program

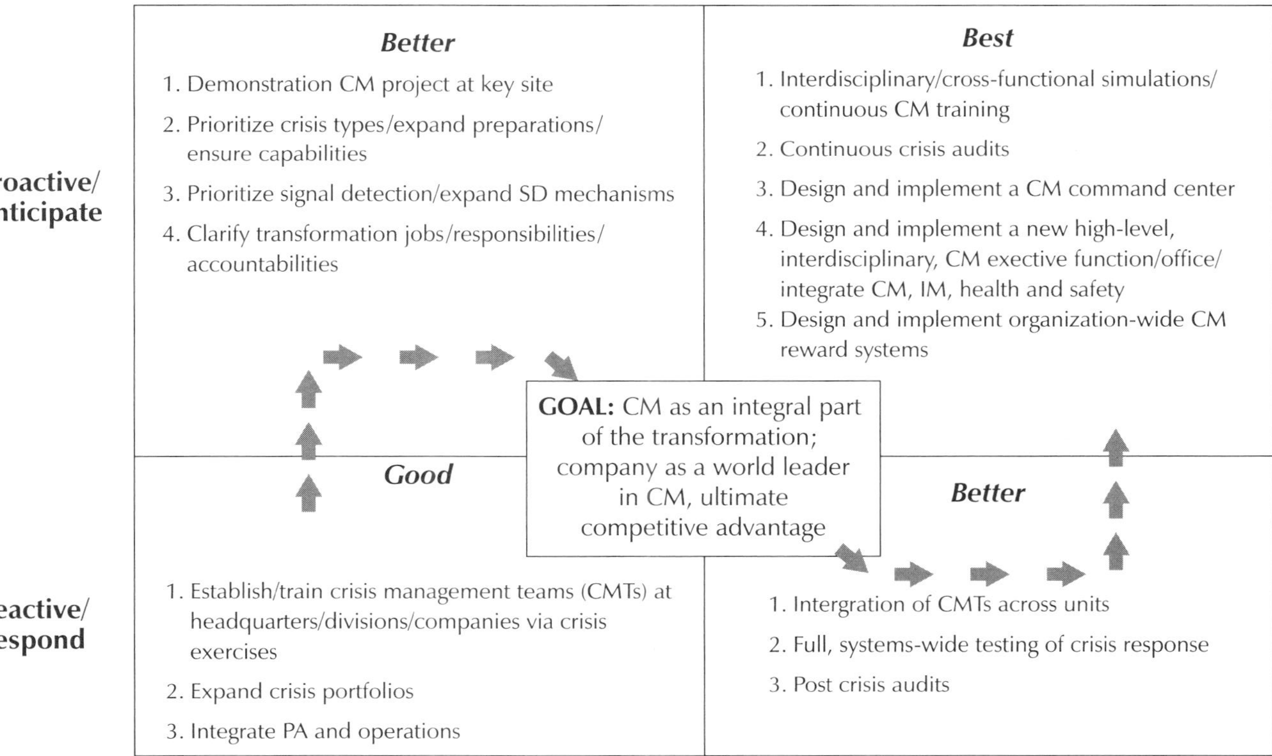

Proactive/ Anticipate
Reactive/ Respond
Better
1. Demonstration CM project at key site
2. Prioritize crisis types/expand preparations/ ensure capabilities
3. Prioritize signal detection/expand SD mechanisms
4. Clarify transformation jobs/responsibilities/ accountabilities
Best
1. Interdisciplinary/cross-functional simulations/ continuous CM training
2. Continuous crisis audits
3. Design and implement a CM command center
4. Design and implement a new high-level, interdisciplinary, CM exective function/office/ integrate CM, IM, health and safety
5. Design and implement organization-wide CM reward systems
GOAL: CM as an integral part of the transformation; company as a world leader in CM, ultimate competitive advantage
Good
1. Establish/train crisis management teams (CMTs) at headquarters/divisions/companies via crisis exercises
2. Expand crisis portfolios
3. Integrate PA and operations
Better
1. Intergration of CMTs across units
2. Full, systems-wide testing of crisis response
3. Post crisis audits

In the end, that which allows us to accept moral responsibility for our actions is the deepest and the highest expression of morality and ethics, i.e., the notion that we are all interconnected, and thereby, bear responsibility for one another. When this idea is finally accepted, then we will have truly taken a giant step in the moral development of humankind.

Strategy List for Chapter Eight

- Recognize that rarely is one single thing or event sufficient to cause another.
- Analyze all contributing factors to get a sense of the Big Picture.
- Map the full array of forces that contribute to your situation to formulate action plans.
- Consult the map to ensure that the corrective actions won't make the crisis worse.
- Use Exhibit 8-4 to help prepare for major crises.

Chapter Nine

Crisis Management 2002

The Challenges Ahead

"The will to win is important, but the will to prepare is vital."

Joe Paterno, football coach

"In the modern world of business it is useless to be a creative original thinker unless you can also sell what you create. Management cannot be expected to recognize a good idea unless it is presented to them by a good salesman."

David M. Ogilvy, advertising guru

2002 will be the twentieth anniversary of the Tylenol poisonings, which is generally acknowledged as the unofficial beginning of modern crisis management. Since 1982, much has been learned about crisis management. Much progress has also been made with regard to the implementation of CM within a variety of organizations. However, a great deal more needs to be learned and to be done.

It is unfortunately still the case that only a small percentage of organizations understand the systemic nature of CM. For this reason, only a small number of organizations understand the necessity of building a comprehensive program of CM, whether it is based on the framework in Chapter Three or one of their own.

Only a small fraction of organizations have learned the necessity of preparing for a broad range of crises. In other words, only a small number have learned the necessity of building and maintaining a broad-based crisis portfolio. In the same vein, only a small number have developed signal detection mechanisms for a range of crises. Only a small proportion of organizations have learned the necessity of continually auditing their culture to determine whether it supports or works against CM. Furthermore, only a small number of organizations do regular and systematic stakeholder analysis, and so on and so on. For this reason, we believe that the field of CM is in need of even further progress.

The vast majority of organizations, if they even have a CM program, have one that is fragmented and piecemeal. The particular area in which the most progress has been made is disaster recovery. Because disaster recovery mainly treats natural and physical disasters, it is thereby the least threatening to organizations psychologically. It also makes the least costly demands on them. But this means that the vast majority of organizations fail to plan beyond the most immediate, the most visible, and the most frequently occurring crises.

Because of the lack of an integrated, systematic, and systemic view of CM, the infamous Y2K came and went after being ballyhooed for years. Because of the lack of a shared perspective, there was a general failure on the part of the public, as well as many corporate executives, to see that the preparations for Y2K were successful *precisely because* wide-scale computing disasters did *not* occur!

> *The preparations of Y2K were successful* precisely because *wide-scale computing disasters did* not *occur!*

As a general rule, those who promoted the potential Y2K crisis failed to plan beyond its nonoccurrence. The CM and various disaster communities failed to convince upper management that Y2K was really a dress rehearsal for the other types of crises that could happen. For this reason, I want to spend the remainder of this chapter on one of the biggest challenges that the field of CM faces. Namely, how does one sell CM more broadly so that organizations will be better prepared in the future?

Gaining Top Management Support for CM

The first recommendation that my colleagues and I offer unequivocally is that organizations generally need to find, to develop, and to cultivate an organizational champion (or champions) at the highest levels of their institutions. Experience demonstrates repeatedly that without a champion nothing significant will occur with regard to *any* major program in an organization. This is especially true with regard to CM. However, even with a champion, there is no guarantee that the appropriate actions that will culminate in an organization being prepared for major crises will be taken. In other words, finding the right champion is necessary, but by itself it is not sufficient.

> *Without a champion nothing significant will occur with regard to* any *major program in an organization. This is especially true with regard to CM.*

This raises the question, "How does one find a champion?" The first and the most obvious persons to look for are those who have already successfully championed other systemwide programs. For instance, one should especially seek out those who have successfully gotten their organizations to adopt total quality management or environmental programs. These programs are a natural starting point since CM, TQM, and environmental programs share many features in common. For instance, CM, TQM, and environmentalism all involve the detection of important signals as to the potential emergence of a crisis, a potential quality defect, or a threat to the environment.

Above all, the process of finding a champion requires creativity and innovation. For instance, my colleagues and I have helped various organizations draft and place ads in their company newsletters. We have especially urged people to use both creativity and humor. For instance, some organizations with whom we have worked have run ads to the effect, "Corporate Champions Needed for Important Program. All Who Are Available, Please Apply!" We have also recommended that those who are interested in promoting CM go to their immediate supervisors and solicit their advice on appropriate candidates to "lead the CM charge."

There are a number of things that one should look for when seeking out a champion. One of the most important is that they have a clear track record with regard to the successful design and implementation of at least one other system-wide program. Above all, a champion must be able to see the Big Picture and to make vital connections among the separate parts, divisions, and programs of an organization. This is especially critical since, as we have emphasized repeatedly, a crisis jumps the separate parts of an organization. One must thereby seek out the broadest thinker in the highest management position possible.

It is important that a champion must either understand all the components of a system-wide CM program, such as the one spelled out in Chapter Three, or have the strong desire to gain this knowledge. A champion also needs to understand and thereby be able to make a strong case to convince fellow top executives how a major crisis will derail the major business objectives of the organization. If anything is key, this is it! CM is not merely to be done for its own sake, but because it can and will severely impact the bottom line.

A champion must also be able to identify clearly the distinct stages and activities in implementing a comprehensive CM program, and be able to identify the various levels of management buy-in required. Furthermore, the champion must be able to think creatively and strategically about how to surmount whatever barriers exist to the implementation of a comprehensive CM program.

The champion must allocate a reasonable budget for CM based on appropriate estimates. I cannot overemphasize the terms "reasonable" and "estimates." There is no way that exact costs can be determined for something as complicated as CM. Indeed, one of the strongest indicators of a crisis-prone culture is that it demands excruciatingly precise estimates before it will undertake any action.

An appropriate CM champion must understand how to sell a complex program throughout a complex organization. This means that he or she must excel at selling a program internally and externally. Therefore, the champion must have strong public relations skills. It is also important, but not imperative, for the champion to have a developed internal and external peer network.

Internally, the job is to sell CM to executives at the champion's level as well as to those both above and beneath that level. In other words, one must sell simultaneously up and down the entire chain of command.

Externally, the champion needs to gain support from executives at the same level in other organizations in one's industry. The reason is that successful selling is not a matter of selling to a single, isolated individual, no matter how powerful that individual may be. In order for any organization to adopt a CM program, signals as to its desirability and necessity must come in simultaneously and persistently from a wide variety of sources.

Another part of a successful strategy for selling CM is to thoroughly understand what has proved successful in selling past programs. This means that one must analyze and understand thoroughly the barriers that have had to be overcome with regard to past programs. In short, what has been learned from past efforts? What was done well? What wasn't done well? What would one do differently and why?

Another critical factor in implementing an effective program of CM is forging linkages between CM and other system-wide programs. My colleagues and I do not believe in either designing, maintaining, or selling CM as a separate stand-alone program. Today's organizations are burdened by far too many critical programs with far too little time and resources to accomplish them. Thus, CM is not only systemic within itself, but it must also be integrated systemically with regard to other key programs. To do this, one must constantly explore and develop the natural linkages between CM and other programs.

The burden is on those selling CM to make the point that an effective CM program will help top executives achieve their personal and business objectives.

Another critical factor in selling CM is the analysis of the personal and business objectives of top management. CM must be put in terms that top management understand and appreciate. The burden is on those selling CM to make the crucial point that an effective CM program will help top executives achieve their personal and business objectives.

Another critical aspect of selling CM is a systematic review of past crises or near misses. The goal of analyzing past crises or near misses is not only to assess an organization's crisis capabilities, but also to further strengthen the case for CM.

For each crisis or near miss, one needs to ask the following questions: What are the organization's strengths and weaknesses with regard to CM? What lessons have been learned? What lessons still need to be learned?

As much as possible, one should also use crises that have affected other organizations in one's industry as powerful supporting material. It obviously also helps if one can show patterns of crises, i.e., how crises are interrelated and can thus set off a chain reaction of further crises.

Concluding Remarks

Throughout this book I have tried to show the systemic nature of CM. In addition, I have tried to show how personal character issues are also critical in successfully implementing a program of CM and doing the right things in the heat of a crisis. I have argued that the culture and the infrastructure of an organization are vital as well.

The vast majority of organizations have not been designed to handle major crises. Most of today's CM programs are add-ons or afterthoughts.

Unfortunately, when all is said and done, the vast majority of organizations have not been designed to handle major crises. Most of today's CM programs are add-ons or afterthoughts. It is little wonder then why such programs are not integrated into or accepted by the "mainstream" of organizations. Continuing to multiply add-ons only creates further complication and confusion.

In summary, if I had to make one major recommendation with which organizations could begin, it would be this: Start by designing and implementing signal detection mechanisms throughout your organization. Start by amplifying the signals that already exist in your organization of impending crises. In many cases, the databases that indicate signals of impending crises may already exist, but they need to be reconceptualized to show their relationship to CM.

To be sure, merely putting in bigger and better signal detection mechanisms is not the whole of the matter, but it is a good starting point. In many ways, the field of CM is just beginning.

Additional Readings

1. Glass, Robert L. *Computing Calamities: Lessons Learned from Products, Projects, and Companies that Failed.* Upper Saddle River, N.J.: Prentice Hall, 1999.
2. Goleman, Daniel. *Emotional Intelligence.* New York: Bantam, 1997.
3. Hartley, Robert. *Marketing Mistakes.* New York: Wiley, 1992.
4. Meyrowitz, Joshua. *No Sense of Place: The Impact of Electronic Media on Social Behavior.* New York: Oxford University Press, 1985.
5. Mitroff, Ian I. *Smart Thinking for Crazy Times: The Art of Solving the Right Problems.* San Francisco: Berrett-Koehler, 1998.
6. Mitroff, Ian I., and Harold A. Linstone. *The Unbounded Mind.* New York: Oxford University Press, 1993.
7. Mitroff, Ian I., Christine M. Pearson, and L. Katharine Harrington. *The Essential Guide to Managing Corporate Crises: A Step-by-Step Handbook for Surviving Major Catastrophes.* New York: Oxford University Press, 1996.
8. Mitroff, Ian I., and Warren Bennis. *The Unreality Industry.* New York: Oxford University Press, 1989.
9. Moore, Thomas. "The Fight to Save Tylenol." *Fortune,* November 29, 1982, p. 44.
10. Pauchant, Thierry C., and Ian I. Mitroff. *Transforming the Crisis-Prone Organization: Preventing Individual, Organi-*

zational, and Environmental Tragedies. San Francisco: Jossey-Bass, 1992.

11. Perez-Pena, Richard. "Airliner Crash Near Pittsburgh: All 131 on USAir Jet Are Killed." *New York Times*, September 9, 1994, p. 1.
12. Shrivastava, Paul. *Bhopal: Anatomy of a Crisis*. Cambridge, Mass.: Ballinger, 1987.

Notes

Chapter One

1. Paul Shrivastava, *Bhopal: Anatomy of a Crisis* (Cambridge, Mass.: Ballinger, 1987).
2. *See* Ian I. Mitroff and Harold A. Linstone, *The Unbounded Mind* (New York: Oxford University Press, 1993); *see also* Ian I. Mitroff, *Smart Thinking for Crazy Times* (San Francisco: Berrett-Koehler Publishers, Inc., 1998).
3. Gus Anagnos, Comprehensive Crisis Management, Manhattan Beach, California; Dr. Judith Clair, Boston College; Dr. Sara Kovoor, University of Colorado at Denver; Dr. Thierry Pauchant, HEC University, Montreal, Canada; and Dr. Chris Pearson, University of North Carolina.

Chapter Two

1. Robert Lee Hotz and Frank Clifford, "A Glitch in the System," *Los Angeles Times*, August 14, 1996, sec. A, p. 13.
2. Thomas Moore, "The Fight to Save Tylenol," *Fortune*, November 29, 1982, p. 44.
3. Ibid.
4. Ibid, p. 49.

5. Ibid.
6. Ibid.
7. Lou Harris, *Inside America* (New York: Vintage Books, 1987).
8. Ian I. Mitroff, Christine M. Pearson, and L. Katharine Harrington, *The Essential Guide to Managing Corporate Crises* (New York: Oxford University Press, 1996).
9. Ibid.

Chapter Three

1. Thierry C. Pauchant and Ian I. Mitroff, *Transforming the Crisis-Prone Organization: Preventing Individual, Organizational, and Environmental Tragedies* (San Francisco: Jossey-Bass, 1992).
2. Ibid.
3. Ibid.
4. Ibid.
5. Ibid.

Chapter Four

1. Josh Getlin, "Suffering Scandal Fatigue," *Los Angeles Times*, October 21, 1998, sec. A, pp. 1, 16.
2. See Ian I. Mitroff, Christine M. Pearson, and L. Katharine Harrington, *The Essential Guide to Managing Corporate Crises* (New York: Oxford University Press, 1996).
3. See, for instance, Joshua Meyrowitz, *No Sense of Place: The Impact of Electronic Media on Social Behavior* (New York: Oxford University Press, 1985); see also Ian I. Mitroff and Warren Bennis, *The Unreality Industry* (New York: Oxford University Press, 1989).

4. Personal communication; GBN Los Angeles Chapter meeting, April 22, 1999.
5. Alvin Toffler, *Future Shock* (New York: Bantam Books, 1971).
6. See J. Luft, "The Johari Window," *Human Relations Training News* 5 (1961): 6–7.
7. David Maraniss, *The Clinton Enigma: A Four-and-a-Half Minute Speech Reveals This President's Entire Life* (New York: Simon & Schuster, 1998).
8. Ken Wilber, *Sex, Ecology, Spirituality: The Spirit of Evolution* (Boston: Shambhala, 1995).
9. Ibid.

Chapter Five

1. "Campaign Textbook: How to Handle a Gaffe," *Time*, November 2, 1998, p. 32.
2. Richard Perez-Pena, "Airliner Crash Near Pittsburgh: All 131 On USAir Jet Are Killed," *New York Times*, September 9, 1994, p. 1.
3. Ian I. Mitroff, *Smart Thinking for Crazy Times: The Art of Solving the Right Problems* (San Francisco: Berrett-Koehler, 1998).
4. Ian I. Mitroff and Warren Bennis, *The Unreality Industry* (New York: Oxford University Press, 1989).
5. Ibid.

Chapter Six

1. Dietrich Dörner, *The Logic of Failure* (Reading, Mass: Perseus Books, 1996), p. 10.

Chapter Seven

1. Randall Sullivan, "A Boy's Life," *Rolling Stone*, October 1, 1998, p. 49.
2. Louis Sahagun, "Boy's Bear Hunt Wish Puts Foundation in Cross Hairs, Animal Activists up in Arms at Make-a-Wish for Allowing Dying Teenager to Kill a Kodiac in Alaska," *Los Angeles Times*, May 11, 1996, sec. A, p. 1.
3. Ian I. Mitroff, Christine M. Pearson, and L. Katharine Harrington, *The Essential Guide to Managing Corporate Crises: A Step-by-Step Handbook for Surviving Major Catastrophes* (New York: Oxford University Press, 1996).
4. See Ian I. Mitroff and Harold A. Linstone, *The Unbounded Mind* (New York: Oxford University Press, 1993).
5. Robert Hartley, *Marketing Mistakes* (New York: Wiley, 1992).
6. Mark H. McCormack, *What They Don't Teach You at the Harvard Business School* (New York: Bantam Doubleday Dell, 1988).
7. Daniel Goleman, *Emotional Intelligence* (New York: Bantam, 1997).
8. Robert L. Glass, *Computing Calamities: Lessons Learned from Products, Projects, and Companies that Failed* (New Jersey: Prentice Hall, 1999), pp. 9, 11.

Chapter Eight

1. Ian I. Mitroff, Christine M. Pearson, and L. Katharine Harrington, *The Essential Guide to Managing Corporate Crises* (New York: Oxford University Press, 1996).
2. Ibid.

About the Authors

Dr. Ian Mitroff is the Harold Quinton Distinguished Professor of Business Policy at Marshall School of Business, University of Southern California. He is also the founder of the USC Center for Crisis Management and President of Comprehensive Crisis Management, a consulting firm that works with Fortune 500 companies, major governmental agencies, and not-for-profit organizations. He is widely recognized as one of the founders of the discipline of crisis management.

In addition to his work in crisis management, Dr. Mitroff has helped organizations design and implement information systems for worldwide market intelligence for new products and services, organizational structures and corporate cultures, international business strategies, and public policy.

He is the author of more than 250 papers and articles and 21 books on a wide range of topics, including crisis management, business policy, corporate culture, contemporary media, current events, foreign affairs, nuclear deterrence, organizational change, spirituality in the workplace, and strategic planning. Among his books are *A Spiritual Audit of Corporate America, Smart Thinking for Crazy Times, The Essential Guide to Managing Corporate Crises, Framebreak,* and *The Unbounded Mind.*

Dr. Mitroff is a frequent keynote speaker at national conventions of professional and public organizations and has lectured to academic, corporate, and government leaders in more than twenty countries. He has appeared on many national radio and television shows, including *Window on Wall Street,* Financial News Network, CNN, and National Public Radio's *Marketplace.* He has been a Fellow of the Academy of Management, President of the International Society for the Systems Sciences (1992–1993), and a Fellow of the American Psychological Association.

Dr. Mitroff earned his B.S., M.S., and Ph.D. from the University of California at Berkeley. He lives in Manhattan Beach, California.

Gus Anagnos is Vice President of Comprehensive Crisis Management (CCM). He is an active researcher in the field of crisis management and is responsible for business development at CCM.

In addition to his work in crisis management, Gus Anagnos has over fifteen years of experience in the private sector. He served a four-year term as CFO for Future Estates, Inc. (a Southern California real estate developer) and founded 2wins Drive-Thru, a successful fast-food business located in Southern California. He is currently on the advisory board of 2wins and directly responsible for business expansion and development.

Gus Anagnos consults to organizations seeking financial advice, organization systems design, and negotiation expertise. He is an active researcher in service quality management. His consulting experience includes service quality management applied specifically to the fast-food industry.

He is a member of various industry associations, including: Society for Human Resource Management, American

Society for Industrial Security, International Facility Management Association, Business and Industry Council of Emergency Planning and Preparedness, and Association of Contingency Planners.

Gus Anagnos is a frequent speaker at national conferences and conventions. He earned his B.S. in finance and economics and his M.B.A. from the University of Southern California. He lives in Hermosa Beach, California.

Acknowledgments for Previously Published Materials (continued from copyright page)

Grateful acknowledgment is made to the following sources for permission to reprint from previously published material. The publisher has made diligent efforts to trace the ownership of all copyrighted material in this volume and believes that all necessary permissions have been secured. If any errors or omissions have inadvertently been made, proper corrections will gladly be made in future editions.

Excerpt from Jonathan Lear, *Open-Minded: Working Out the Logic of the Soul,* Cambridge, Mass.: Harvard University Press. Copyright © 1998 by the President and Fellows of Harvard College. Reprinted by permission of the publisher.

Excerpt from Alfred North Whitehead, *Dialogues,* Little, Brown and Company. [1954] Reprinted by permission.

Excerpt from Robert Lee Hotz and Frank Clifford, "A Glitch in the System," *Los Angeles Times,* August 14, 1996. Copyright © 1996, *Los Angeles Times.* Reprinted by permission.

Excerpt from Thomas Moore, "The Fight to Save Tylenol," *Fortune,* November 29, 1982, pp. 44, 49. Copyright © 1982 Time Inc. Reprinted by permission.

Excerpt from Louis Harris, *Inside America,* New York: Vintage Books, a division of Random House, 1987.

Excerpt from Josh Getlin, "Suffering Scandal Fatigue," *Los Angeles Times,* October 21, 1998. Copyright © 1998, *Los Angeles Times.* Reprinted by permission.

Excerpt from "Campaign Textbook: How to Handle a Gaffe," *Time,* November 2, 1998, p. 33. Copyright © 1998, Time Inc. Reprinted by permission.

Excerpt from interview with Peter Schwartz. Permission courtesy of Peter Schwartz.

Excerpt from Dietrich Dörner, *The Logic of Failure,* translated by Rita and Robert Kimber, © 1996 by Metropolitan Books. Reprinted by permission of Henry Holt & Co., LLC.

Excerpt from Randall Sullivan, "A Boy's Life, Part 2," *Rolling Stone,* October 1, 1998. Quote by Randall Sullivan from *Rolling Stone,* October 1, 1998, by Straight Arrow Publishers Company, LP. 1998. All rights Reserved. Reprinted by permission.

Excerpt from Louis Sahagun, "Boy's Bear-Hunt Wish Puts Foundation in Cross Hairs," *Los Angeles Times,* May 11, 1996. Copyright © 1996, *Los Angeles Times.* Reprinted by permission.

Excerpt from Robert L. Glass, *Computing Calamities: Lessons Learned from Products, Projects, and Companies That Failed,* Upper Saddle River, N. J.: Prentice-Hall, 1999, pp. 9, 11.

Index